Siona

The Cleveland Art Museum
May 95

Between Past and Present: French, English, and American Etching 1850-1950

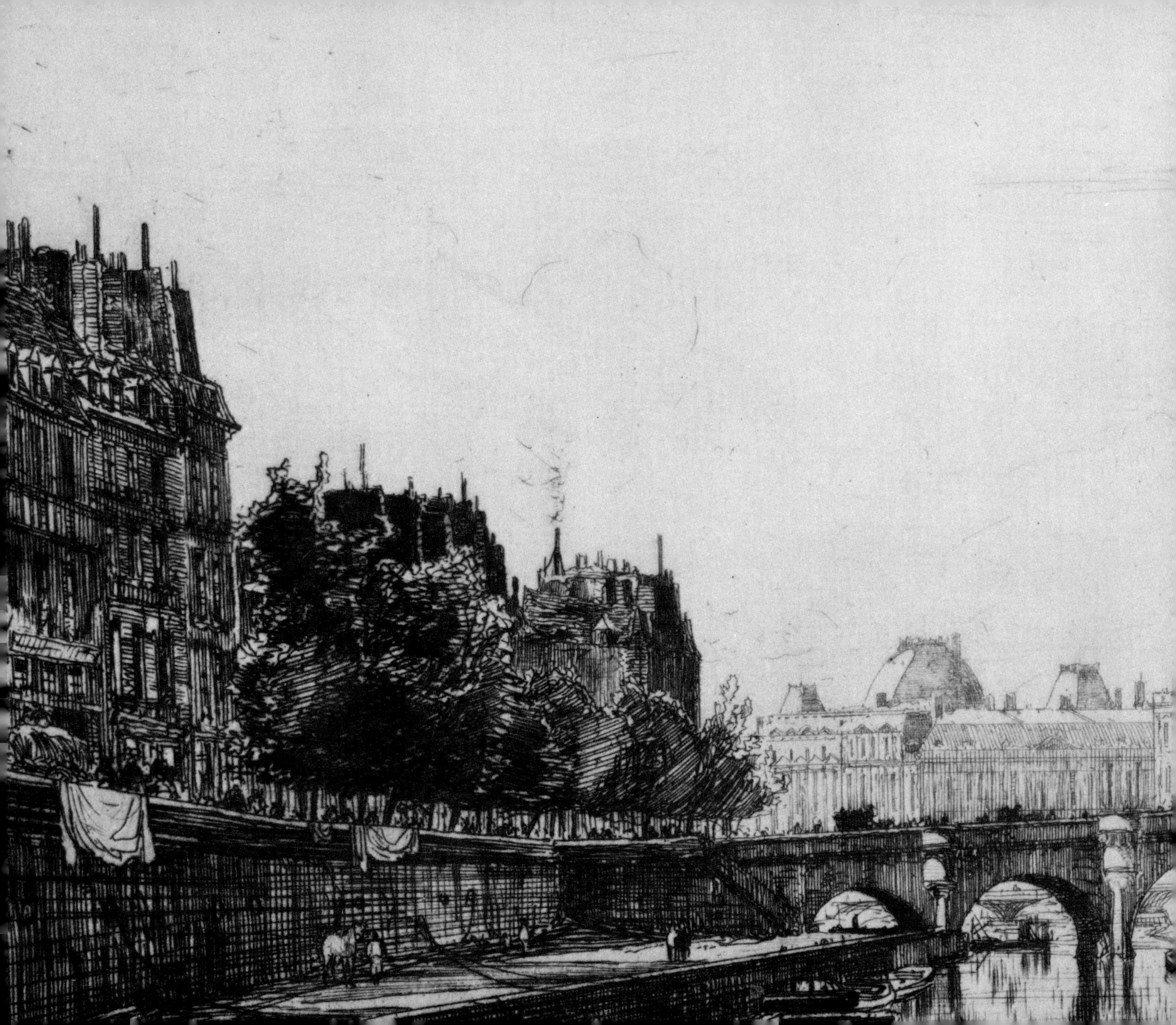

Between Past and Present: French, English, and American Etching 1850-1950

Gabriel P. Weisberg

Ronnie L. Zakon

Published by The Cleveland Museum of Art
in cooperation with
The Federal Reserve Bank of Cleveland

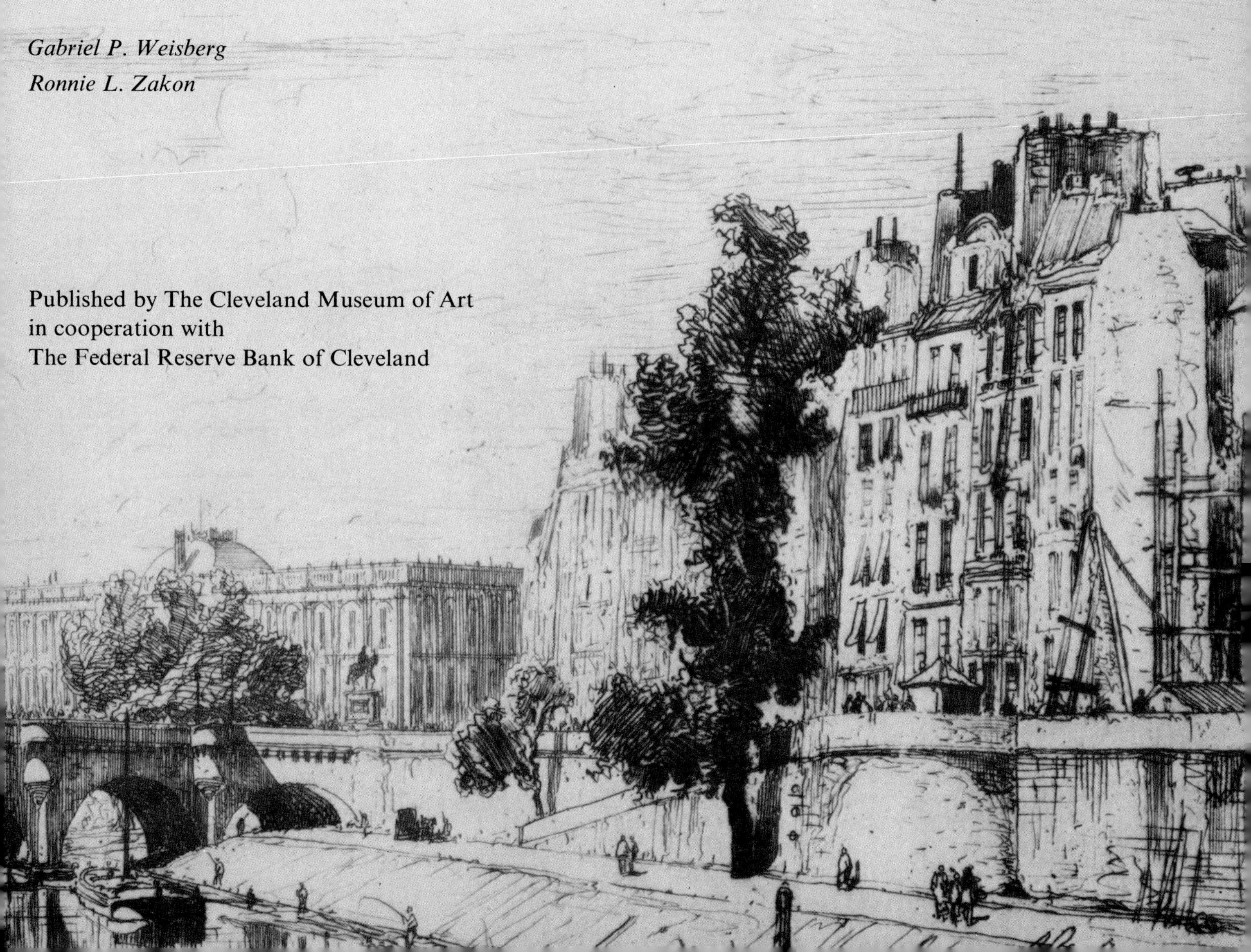

Lenders

Associated American Artists
The Cleveland Museum of Art,
    Prints and Drawings Department
The Cleveland Museum of Art,
    Extensions Division of the
    Department of Art History and Education
The College of Wooster

Copyright 1977 by The Cleveland Museum of Art
Library of Congress Catalog Card Number 76-53113
ISBN   910386-33-1

Preface

Between Past and Present: French, English, and American Etching 1850-1950 examines artists who reached a peak of popularity during the 1920's and 1930's. At that time, periodicals, art dealers, and wealthy collectors eagerly supported etchers who recorded a leisurely atmosphere, centering on fashionable locales or oft-visited monuments. The works of these printmakers frequently were collected not for their intrinsic qualities but because audiences nostalgically idolized Paris, Venice, or London.

It is only in recent times—as an understanding of prior attitudes and tastes has developed—that "forgotten" etchers have been revived. Instead of seeing these earlier printmakers as recorders of nostalgic voyages, younger collectors and critics have become aware that their images reveal themes affecting painters, sculptors, and architects who sought to recapture qualities of the past in a rapidly changing present. Often the charm of an etcher's picturesque impression or the romantic solitariness of a print demonstrates how qualities can be personalized for a contemporary audience eager to understand quieter messages from the past. In this way a deeper awareness of tastes can be studied; changes in previous attitudes can be grasped as a foundation for the "new" attitudes of a younger audience.

The exhibition would not have been realized without the assistance of many individuals. In New York unusual etchings were obtained from Associated American Artists, whose director, Sylvan Cole, responded enthusiastically to the concept of the show. Other prints were secured from a private collector; from the Cleveland Museum's Prints and Drawings Department and the Extensions Division of the Department of Art History and Education; and The College of Wooster.

The preparation of the installation and publication of the catalogue were aided by many, including: Andrew T. Chakalis, Supervisor, Extensions Division, Department of Art History and Education; Merald Wrolstad of the Publications Department, who designed the catalogue; Martin Linsey and Nickolas Hlobeczy, who prepared the photographs of the objects in the show; Sally Goodfellow, who assisted with preliminary matters; Willis J. Winn, President, Federal Reserve Bank of Cleveland, who encouraged the project in many ways; Louise S. Richards, Curator of Prints and Drawings; and Museum Director Sherman E. Lee, who read the manuscript at various stages, providing valuable suggestions. Ronnie Zakon, instructor in the Department of Art History and Education, worked diligently on the selection of prints and wrote the incisive biographies on each artist.

Gabriel P. Weisberg, Curator
Department of Art History and Education

Contents

Photographic Credits

Martin Linsey, Staff Photographer,
   Department of Art History and Education
The Cleveland Museum of Art Photography Studio

Introduction

Since the middle of the seventeenth century, etchers in various countries developed an increasing intimacy with their environment. As painters studied nature, so printmakers—Rembrandt and others in Holland—immersed themselves in effects of light and climate on the external world. Often they recorded the cottages of the people; they gave an accurate view of the landscape and the changing effects that the seasons had upon the world they found themselves living in. Landscape printmaking, beginning in the sixteenth century, gained from Dutch printmakers who travelled throughout their country recording pathways and natural effects. When this tradition was transplanted to England during the course of the eighteenth century, printmakers immediately found themselves developing an iconographic scheme: they repeated the motif of the old cottage, a mountain view, or trees in the depths of a forest. These traditions eventually developed into the "picturesque"—a predecessor of romantic theory—where printmakers immersed themselves in a study of the world and increased the spectrum of usable themes as a further dimension of a romantic sensibility.

In the nineteenth century, as artists found themselves alienated by progress and industrial technology, they returned to the quieter traditions established in the seventeenth and eighteenth centuries. Their romantic commitment to nature was tinged with memories of the picturesque—a love of ruins and architectural monuments from previous times—which they found comforting and consoling. Printmakers, at mid-century, reacquainted themselves with the countryside, travelling by boat or on foot to find a quiet, desolate location where they could commune with themselves and their undesecrated environment. Etching—a deeply personal medium—permitted them to record their sympathies more intimately than in other art forms.

In the process of this reexamination of the world in which they found themselves, etchers from France, England, and the United States shared similarities. Not the least of the themes with which they worked was the country view as opposed to the cityscape—reiterating one of the basic conflicts of the period 1850-1950 when printmakers (in microcosm) reflected the deeper changes affecting European art.

By isolating the differing thematic categories that printmakers used, it will be possible to see how a universal viewpoint was found in prints from many countries. Often the prints reflected a tendency to look toward the past; in fact, prints maintained a more traditional grasp of thematic concepts for a longer period than was found in painting of the the same time. It is to the exploration of this theory that this exhibition devotes itself.

BIBLIOGRAPHY

Selected General Bibliography

Béraldi, Henri. *Les Graveurs du XIXe Siècle*. Paris, 1885-1892.

Bibliothèque Nationale. *Inventaire du Fonds Français après 1800*. Paris, 1971.

Bradley, William A. *French Etchers of the Second Empire*. New York, 1916.

Cate, Phillip Dennis. "Reviving Forgotten Printmakers of the 19th Century." *Art News* 73 (March 1974): 53-56.

Clark, Kenneth. *The Gothic Revival*. London, 1949.

Hamerton, Philip. *Etching and Etchers*. London, 1868.

Hussey, Christopher. *The Picturesque: Studies in a Point of View*. London and New York, 1927.

Kovler Gallery. *Forgotten Printmakers of the 19th Century*. Chicago, 1967.

Weisberg, Gabriel P. *The Etching Renaissance in France: 1850-1880*. Salt Lake City: Utah Museum of Fine Arts, 1971.

I. ENVIRONMENT: RURAL AND CITY

A. Country Views

With the revival of etching in France during the 1860's, under the sponsorship of the Société des Aquafortistes, printmakers moved outside and worked directly from the images which confronted their eyes. Among those who served as an important initiator of new trends in printmaking was Félix Bracquemond (1833-1914) whose interest in light effects and the sparkling reflections of water served as a starting point for his Impressionist colleagues.

Bracquemond found secluded locations—*Les Saules des Mottiaux* [1]—where the heat of a summer afternoon did not disturb the quiet contemplation of such a scene. Bracquemond's innate romanticism led him to select this location; his commitment toward scenes of meditation anticipate what was to come in French art and reiterate the printmaker's love of nature which was happily rediscovered during the 1850's. A second etching—*Le Bateau du Teinturier (Bas-Meudon)* [2]—helps in placing Bracquemond among those artists who travelled throughout the countryside (often with notebook or copper plate in hand) so as to record their spontaneous reaction to the changing scene. Suggesting ties with the landscapist Charles Daubigny, Bracquemond helps to show that many artists were eager to escape from the city to work by themselves in the quiet of a small inlet or in a provincial locale.

Maxime Lalanne (1827-1886), also a member of the Société des Aquafortistes, emerged from the tradition of studying nature by recording differing views observed on trips. His early works, often sketchbook drawings, show how he studied decaying ruins or focused on a cascading waterfall as part of his love of the picturesque countryside of France. Lalanne's later prints—while frequently set within the confines of the city—occasionally record his fondness for the waterways of the country. *The Canal at Pont-Sainte-Maxence* [3] links him with Bracquemond in an attempt to find a peaceful scene where strollers could walk on a quiet riverbank.

A third member of the Société des Aquafortistes, Adolphe Appian (1818-1898), was not only a Salon painter of large-scale compositions in the Barbizon tradition, but a printmaker who continued in his prints the use of desolate streams and isolated beaches [4 and 5]. Undoubtedly Appian's prints were widely available, often reproducing one of his recent Salon triumphs. They completed the idea of spreading the country view to provincial areas of France.

At the same time that the romantic country view was being used in France, English printmakers—among them Francis Seymour Haden (1818-1910)—demonstrated that the same interest in nature could be applied to the English countryside. A similar attention to light and atmosphere and an increasing understanding that the pure contemplation of nature meant the elimination of man from the image was paramount. Personal thoughts emanated from the study of a small pond [6]; man had to find tranquillity once again by observing his environment anew, almost with innocent eyes, and grasp the fact that nature was always present, following ever-recurring cycles which no industrialization of the country could erase. A similar fondness for isolated locales, with a broad sweeping vista—recalling the magnitude of an untarnished land—are found in the prints of a later Scottish artist, D. Y. Cameron [7].

While many of the artists of the mid-century knew one another personally and often saw each other's works exhibited in the same gallery or exposition, the maintenance of the universal importance of contemplating nature was transmitted to another artist often without any personal contact. John Taylor Arms (1887-1953), an American, has very close affinities with many of the French and English printmakers of mid-century. Aware of their images and often dedicated to their theories, Arms travelled throughout the world becoming a twentieth-century reincarnation of the picturesque voyager. His etchings of Italian landscapes [8]—from the 1920's—not only realistically record what he actually saw but demonstrate his late romantic sensitivity to the countryside and to staggering glimpses of nature. Although modern inroads did appear, such as the telephone wires in *Saint Paul, Alpes Maritime* [9], it was the dominant effect of the old city with its associations from the past which led Arms to study the shapes in the first place. Even a late print, *Cavendish Common* [10], lends support to the belief that an underlying philosophy affected certain printmakers. Even when man's buildings became the major attraction, the wide expanse surrounding the forms underscores that they were part of a larger scheme connected in a printmaker's mind with rural passages evoking a quieter, less frenetic world than the one found in the 1940's.

Félix Bracquemond, French, 1833-1914.

1 *The Willows on the Mottiaux (Les Saules des Mottiaux).*
Etching, 1868. 8 x 11-5/8 inches (20.3 x 29.5 cm.).
Béraldi number 190, iii. Lent by Associated American Artists, New York.

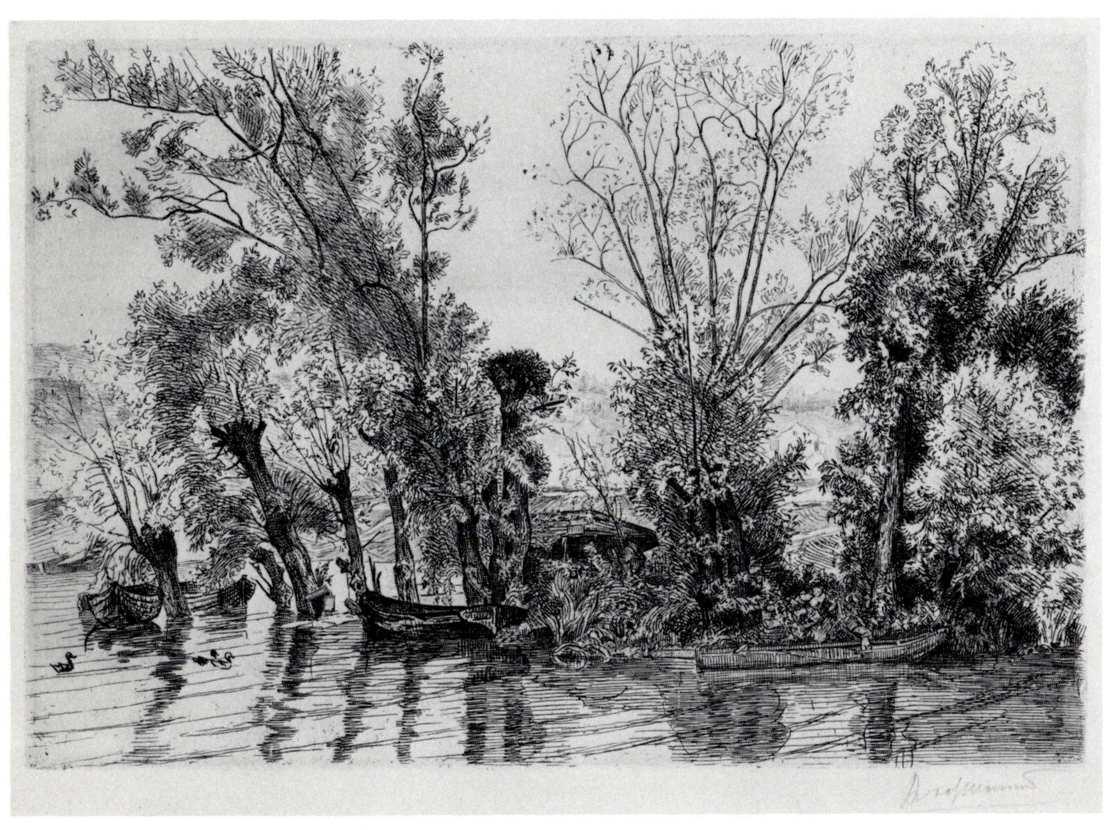

Félix Bracquemond.

2 *The Dyer's Boat (Bas-Meudon)*
(Le Bateau du Teinturier, Bas-Meudon).
Etching, 1868.
6-3/8 x 4-3/4 inches
(16.2 x 12.1 cm.).
Béraldi number 192.
Collection of Dr. and Mrs.
Gabriel P. Weisberg, Cleveland.

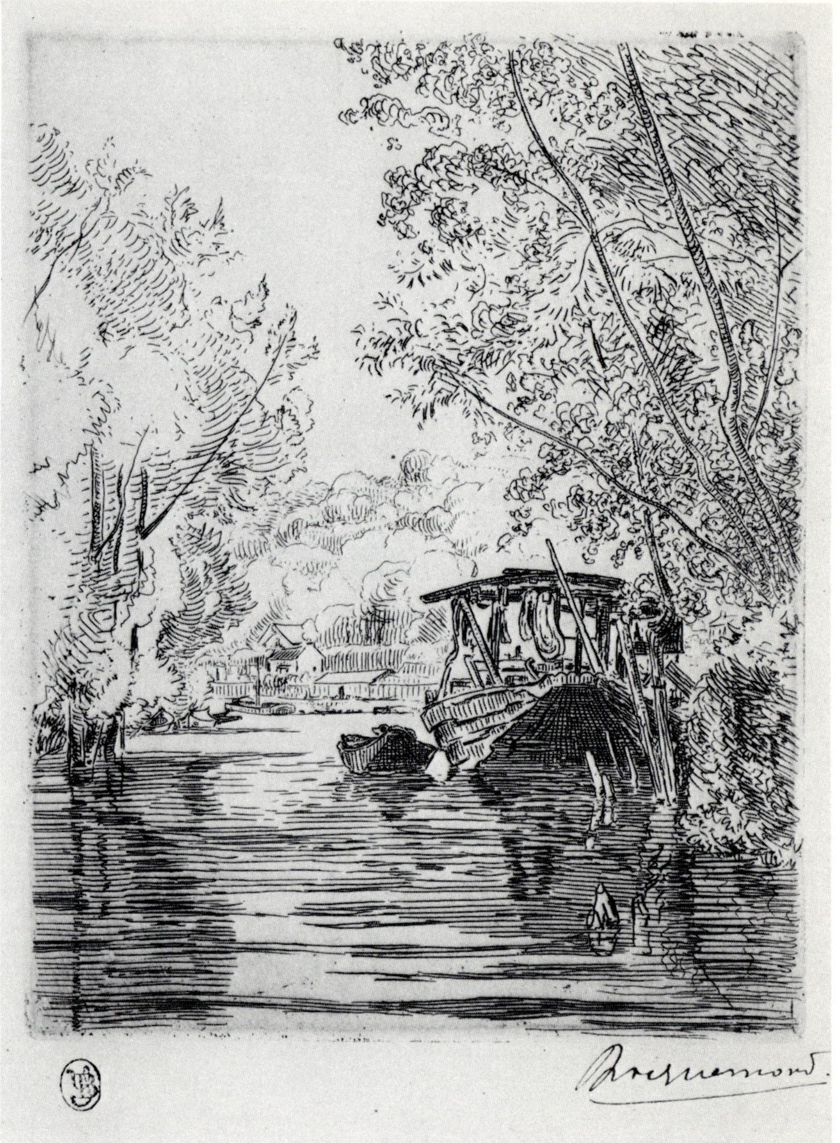

Maxime Lalanne, French, 1827-1886.

3 *The Canal at Pont-Sainte-Maxence.*
Etching, undated. 9-3/16 x 6-3/4 inches (23.4 x 17.1 cm.).
Béraldi number 88. Bequest of John L. Severance. CMA 42.745

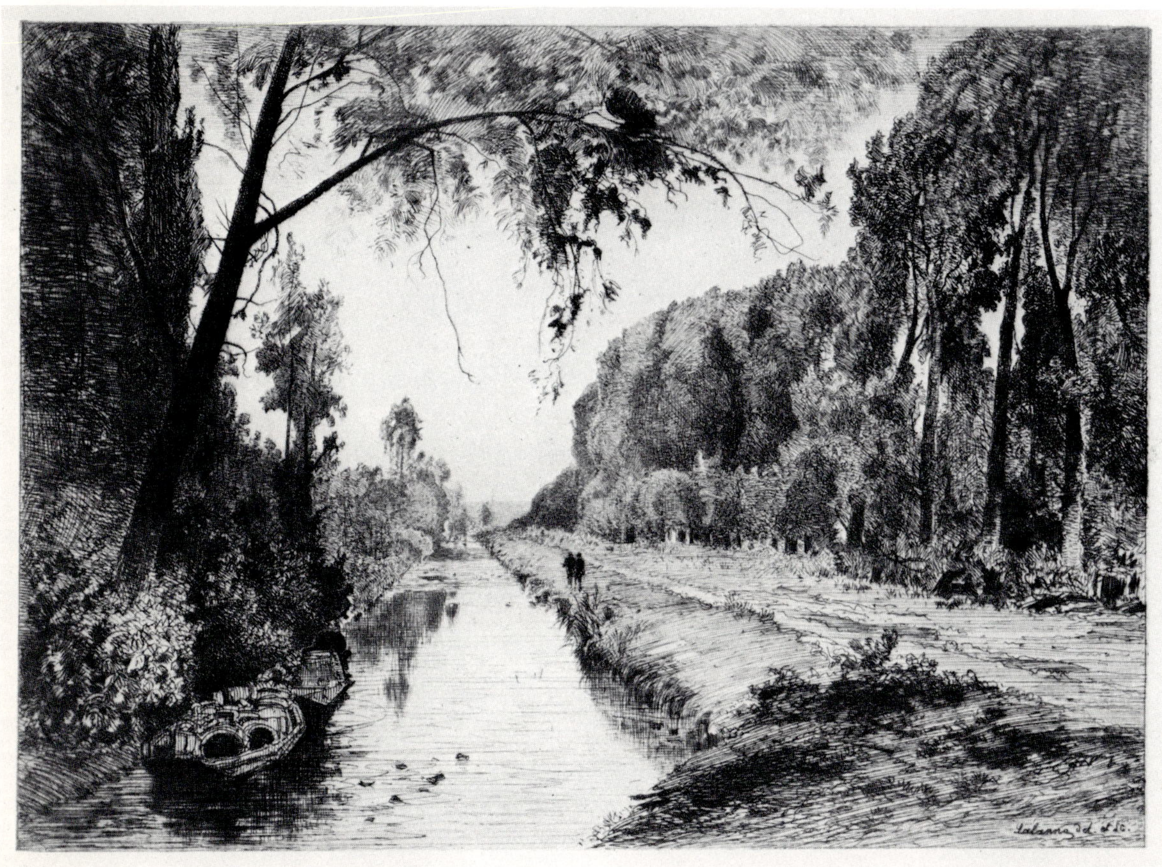

Adolphe Appian, French, 1818-1898.

4 *At Valromey (Au Valromey).*

Etching, 1868. 4 x 7-1/2 inches (10.2 x 19 cm.).
Curtis and Prouté number 25, ii. Lent by Associated American Artists, New York.

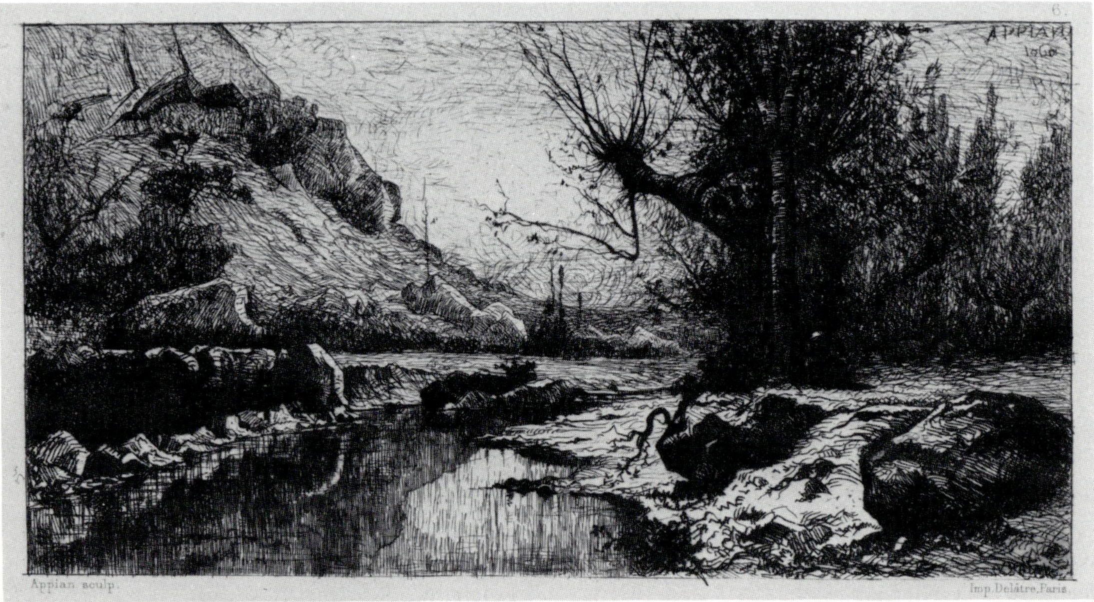

Adolphe Appian.

5 *Environs of Carqueronne (Environs de Carqueronne).*
Etching, 1882. 5-5/8 x 9-5/8 inches (14.3 x 24.4 cm.).
Curtis and Prouté number 60, i. Lent by Associated American Artists, New York.

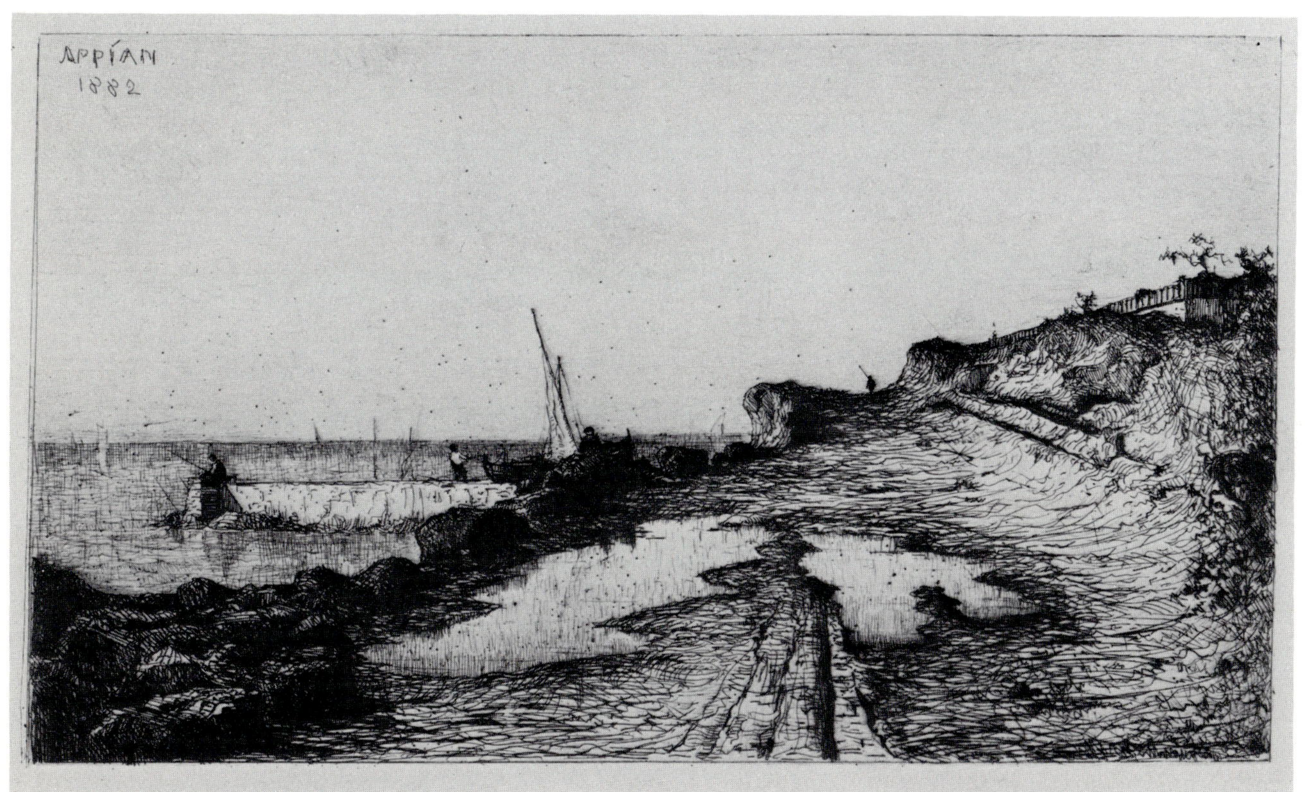

Francis Seymour Haden, English, 1818-1910.

6 *Shere Mill Pond* (Large Plate).
Etching, 1860. 7 x 13-1/8 inches (17.8 x 33.3 cm.).
Harrington number 38. Gift of Leonard C. Hanna, Jr. CMA 47.402

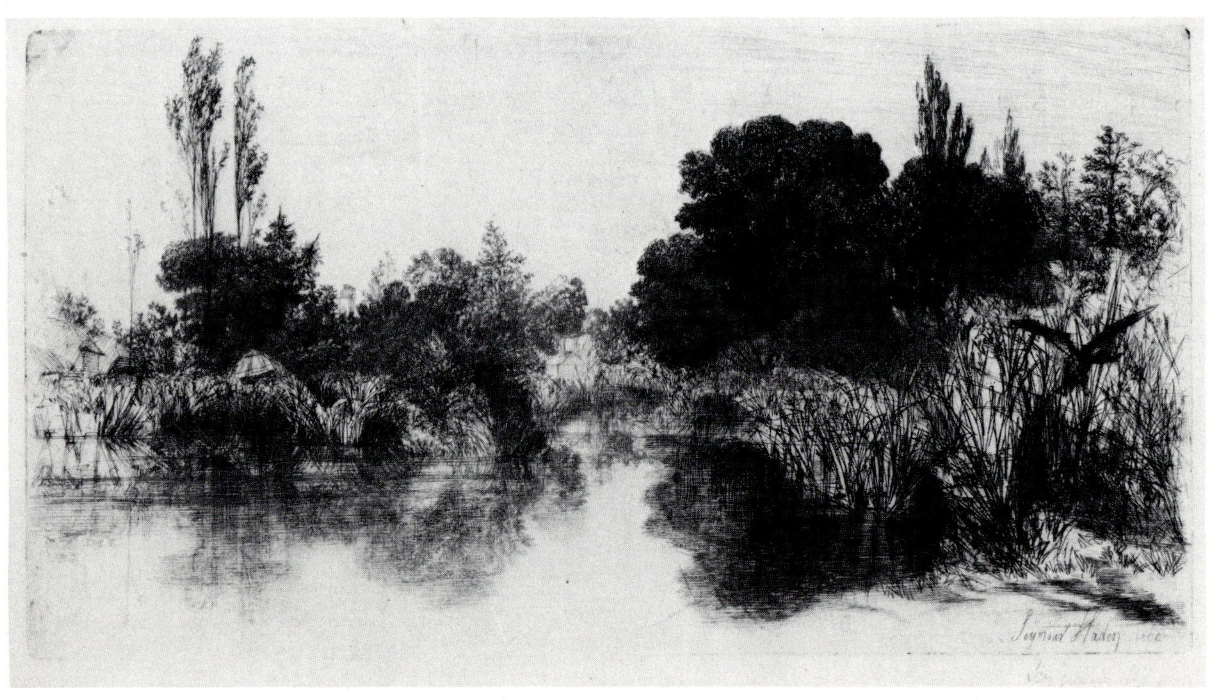

D. Y. Cameron, Scottish, 1865-1945.

7 *Landscape.*
Etching, undated. 6-7/8 x 16-5/8 inches (17.5 x 42.2 cm.).
Lent by The College of Wooster.

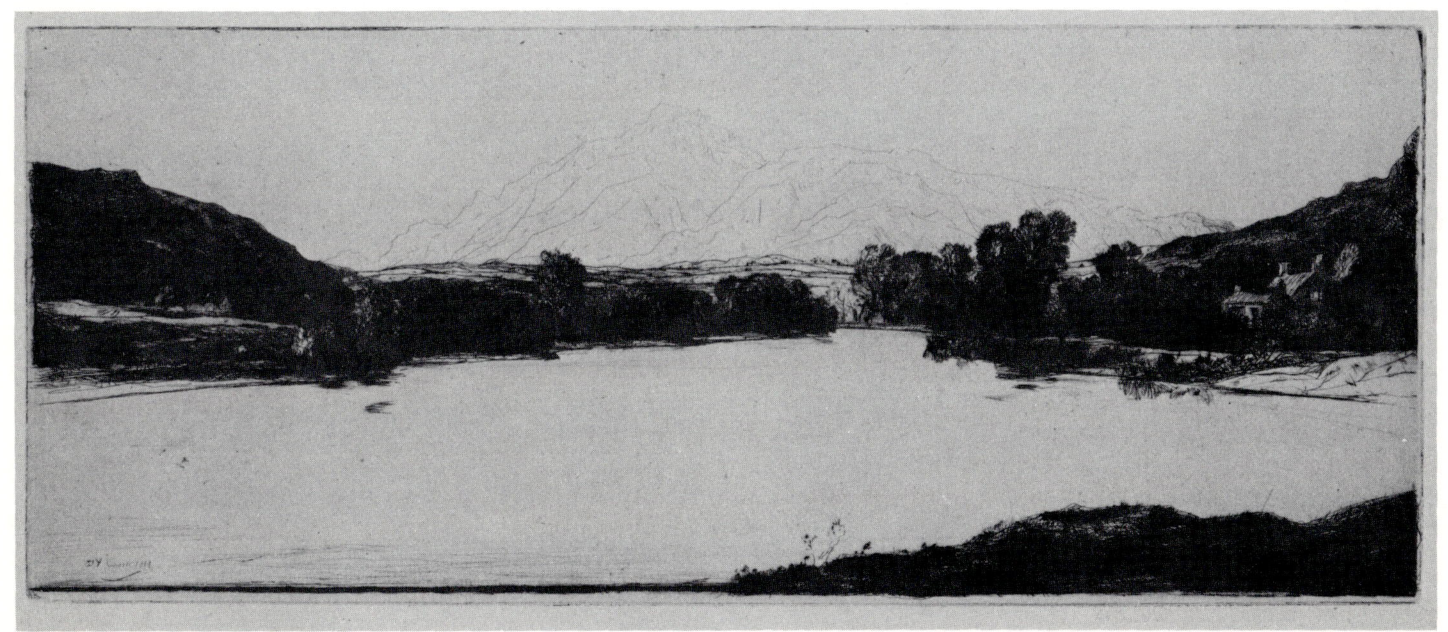

John Taylor Arms,
American, 1887-1953.

8 *Grim Orvieto*.
Etching, 1926.
11-1/8 x 8-5/8 inches
(28.2 x 21.9 cm.).
American Etchers,
Volume V, number 110.
Lent by Associated
American Artists,
New York.

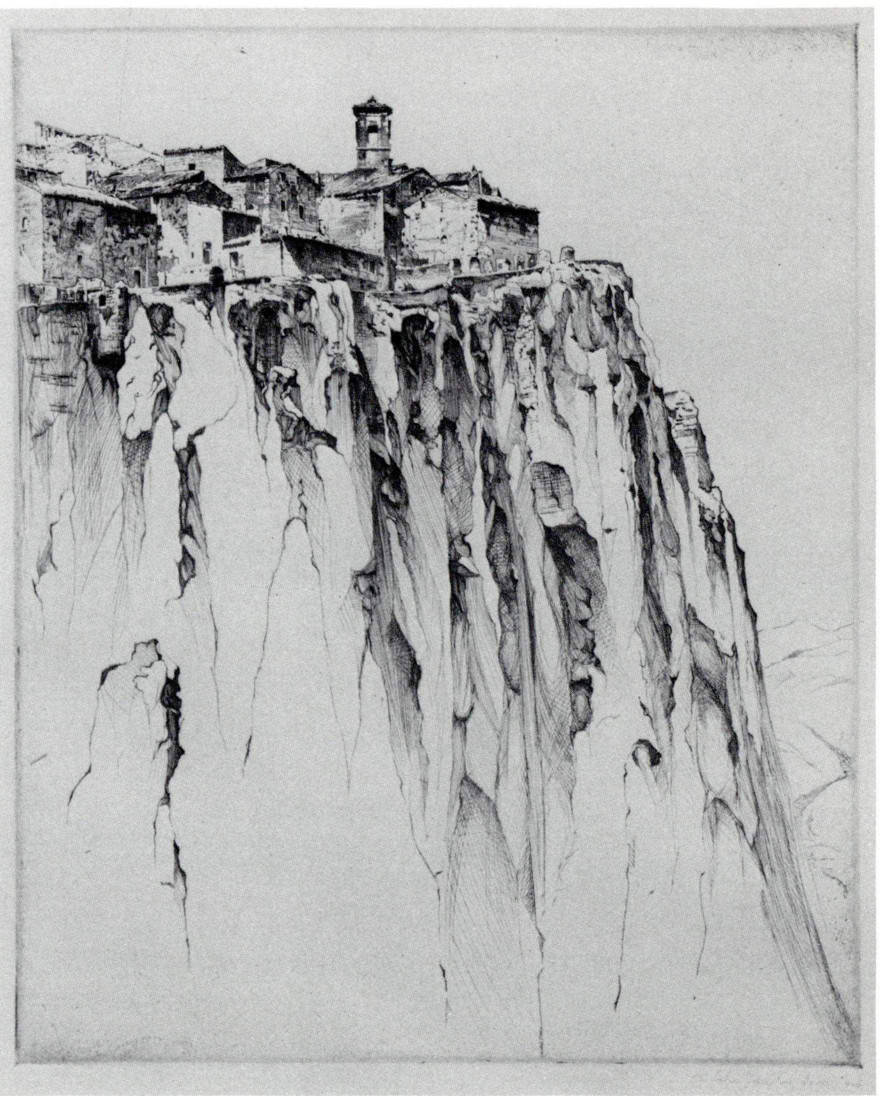

John Taylor Arms.

9 *Saint Paul, Alpes Maritimes.*

Etching, 1927. 7-5/8 x 11-9/16 inches (19.3 x 29.3 cm.).
American Etchers, Volume V, number 131. Gift of The Print Club. CMA 33.231

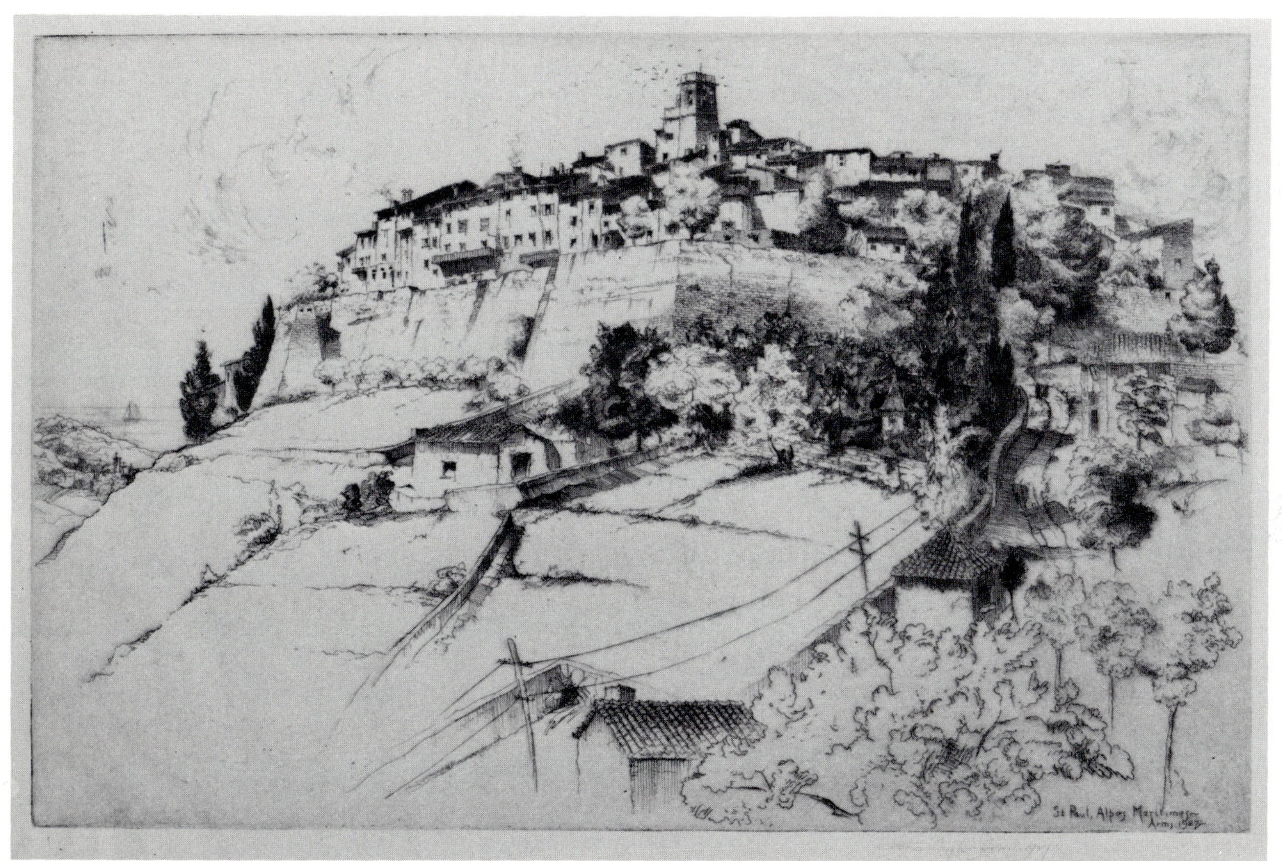

John Taylor Arms.

10 *Cavendish Common.*
Etching, 1942. 5-1/2 x 14-5/8 inches (14 x 37.1 cm.).
Kennedy Galleries number 82. Lent by Associated American Artists, New York.

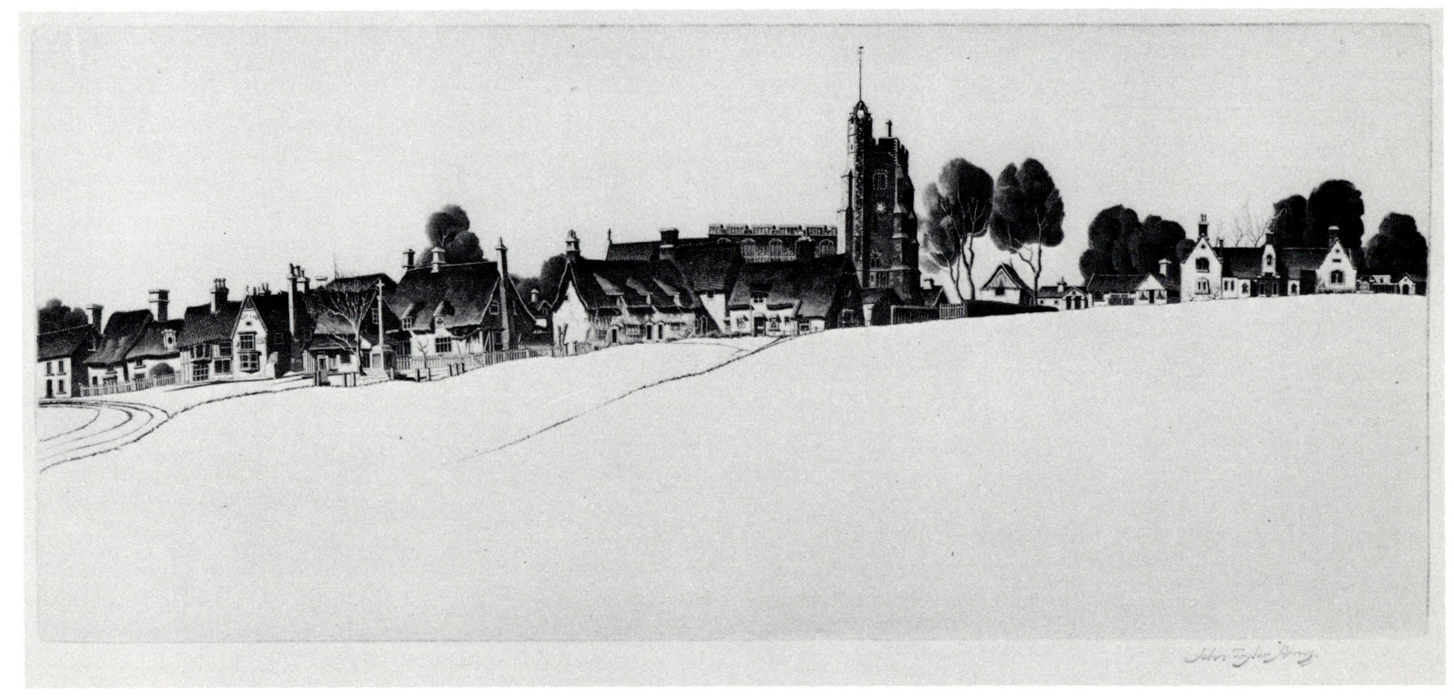

I. ENVIRONMENT: RURAL AND CITY

B. River Views

The same attention given to the solitary countryside was often centered around rivers or harbors—locales which some printmakers found had the same quality of isolation and loneliness. By extending the landscape to the city, printmakers from mid-century on were haunted by memories of their own experiences along the banks of a river which they often found transformed by new buildings and piers. In answer to the changes taking place through man's control of his environment, printmakers in France, England, and America quietly evoked the charm of a Venetian canal or drew back to expose how a river had been tamed by the presence of stone quais or massive bridges. The innocent, undisturbed beauty of nature—available through solitary walks through the country—was lost when a river wandered through a changed industrialized city. Just as painters longed for a simpler existence, so etchers yearned for moments of repose —in communion with rivers—which were not possible as society changed the face of its waterways.

Among those etchers who saw the river as a harbinger of romantic moods was the lonely Charles Meryon (1821-1868). Obsessed by the ancient architecture of Paris, Meryon was also haunted by the presence of the Seine which provided an age-old link with past associations and traditions. *L'Arche du Pont Notre-Dame, Paris* [11] evokes the earlier prints of Piranesi while thrusting one into the teeming river life of a city filled with picturesque monuments. The activity of the figures is unimportant as they are dwarfed by the gigantic size of the architecture and the disquieting presence of a bridge which overwhelms the river. Meryon's darkening mood evokes a feeling of regret that man's buildings impinge on the river's life. The artist forces us to look beyond the con-fines of the bank, as does one small figure who scales a rope.

Not all the printmakers of the period presented such a disconsolate view of river existence as did Meryon. Maxime Lalanne's *Vue Prise du Pont Saint Michel* [12] objectively records a similar locale where the stately activity of river work continues in a city brilliantly illuminated on a summer day. The same attention paid trees is now extended to the quais along the Seine—man's habitat—as these shapes begin to replace a fondness for mountains and trees. Félix Bracquemond in *Le Pont Alexandre III* [13] found a far more exuberant response to the city's relationship with its river as he filled his image with light and air, drawing back from a confining examination of the bridges of Paris to see the city from a cosmic realm. The presence of the small boat steaming jauntily up the Seine and the Eiffel Tower, in the back, suggests a bright new era for the inhabitants of the city. Created after the Impressionist exhibitions, Bracquemond tried to underscore that existence was not totally bleak if one looked about the city and observed seasonal changes over the river.

Aside from these momentary glimpses of equilibrium, the vast number of prints created by artists in the latter part of the century maintain a type of romantic melancholy. Often etchers recorded solitary boats, moored near a wharf [14], with the presence of human beings minimized. When artists went to new locales—Venice, for example [15-17]—they may have been interested in recording leisure activity as much as the changes implicit in a river view. What they did find was a picturesque new region which helped to reaffirm the importance of travel for artists drawing on themes from their environment.

American printmakers also responded to the same theme:

witness the images of Joseph Pennell—best known for his
industrial scenes—[18-19] who selected isolated boats or
projected a cosmic view—similar to Bracquemond—over the
Thames. Thus, whenever the opportunity arose, the printmaker tried to extend his vocabulary by focusing on the river.
Often the innocent qualities which had been preferred from
an earlier age were tempered to meet the changes wrought by
man in remolding his environment to meet the demands of
the machine age.

Charles Meryon, French, 1821-1868.

11 *An Arch of the Notre-Dame Bridge (L'Arche du Pont Notre-Dame, Paris).*

Etching, 1853. 5 x 6-9/16 inches (12.7 x 16.6 cm.).

Delteil and Wright number 25, iv. Gift of The Print Club. CMA 22.147

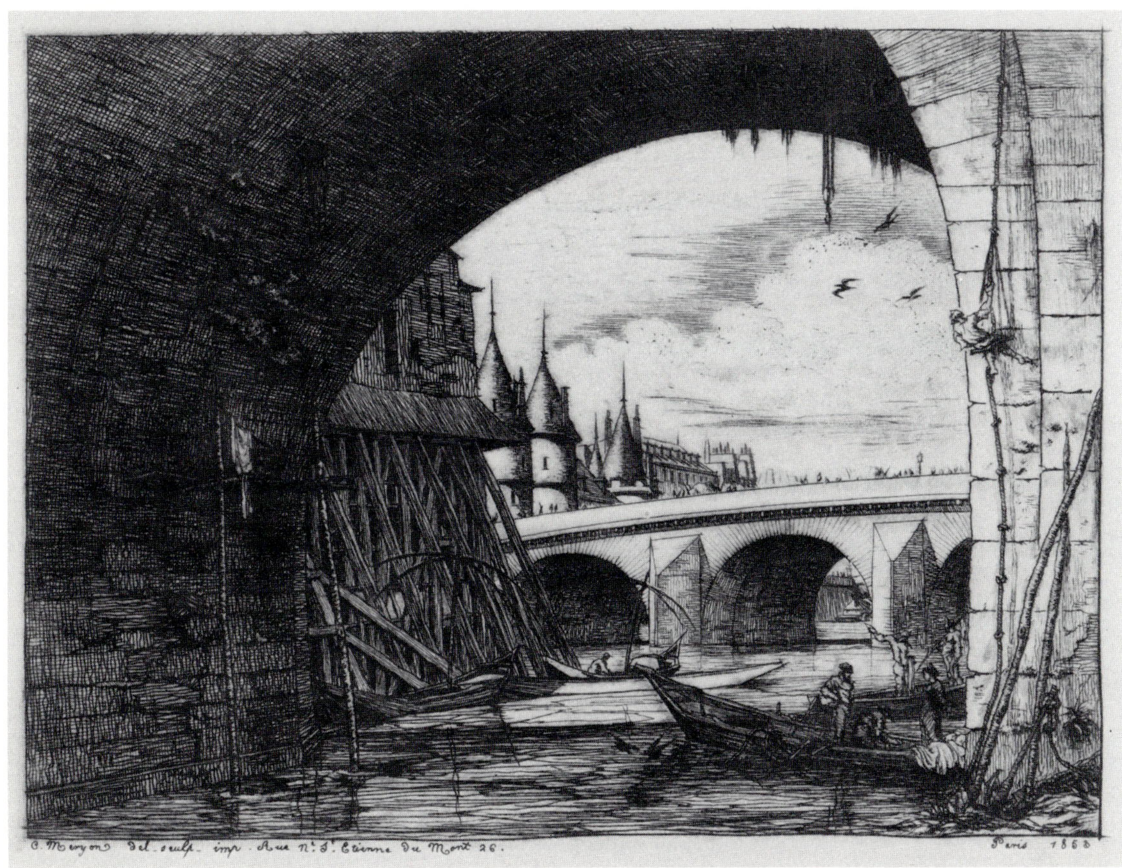

Maxime Lalanne.

12 *View from The Saint-Michel Bridge (Vue Prise du Pont Saint-Michel).*
Etching, undated. 9-7/16 x 12-5/8 inches (24 x 32 cm.).
Béraldi number 8. Gift of Mr. Ralph King. CMA 20.691

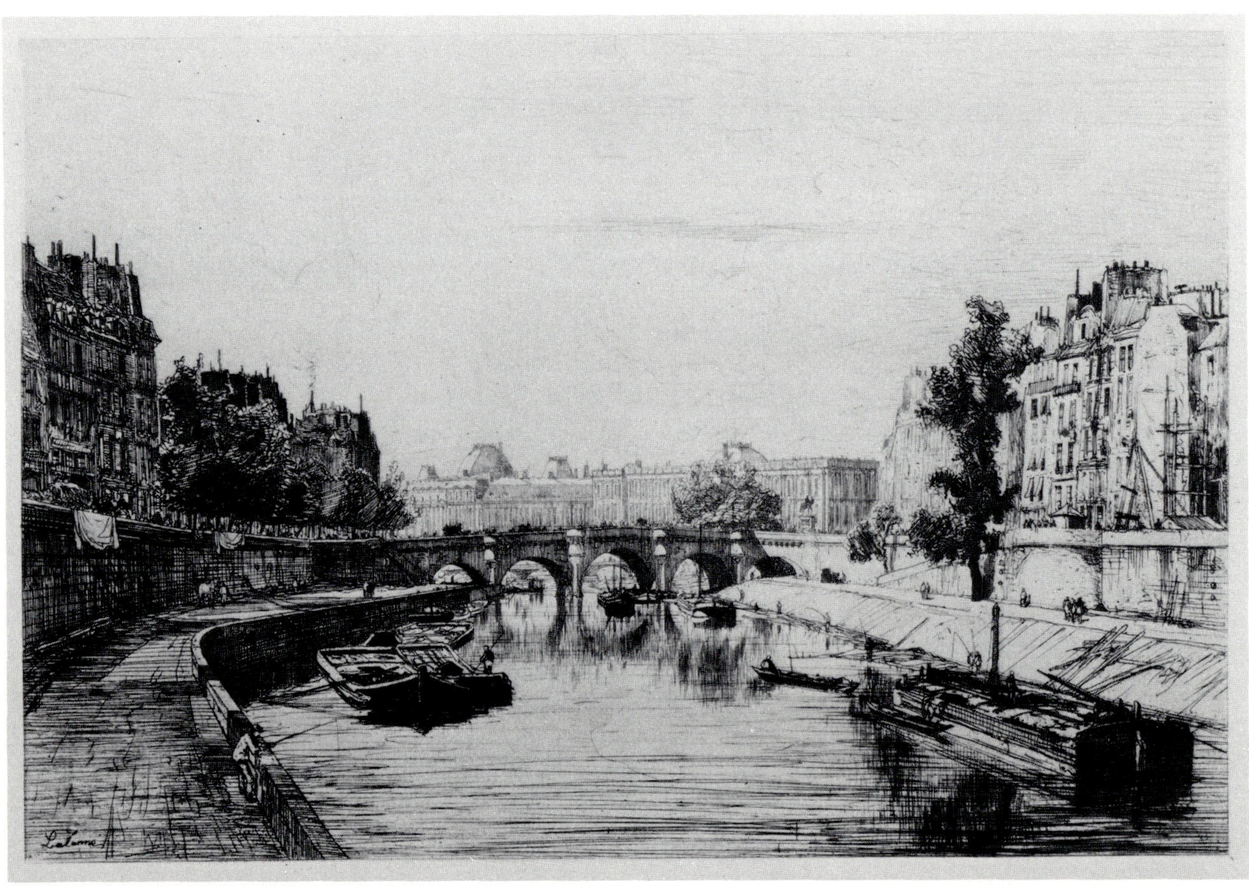

Félix Bracquemond.

13 *The Alexander III Bridge*
(Le Pont Alexandre III).
Etching, undated.
11-1/4 x 8-5/8 inches
(28.6 x 21.9 cm.).
Inventaire du Fonds
Français après 1800,
Tome 3, number 473.
Lent by Associated
American Artists,
New York.

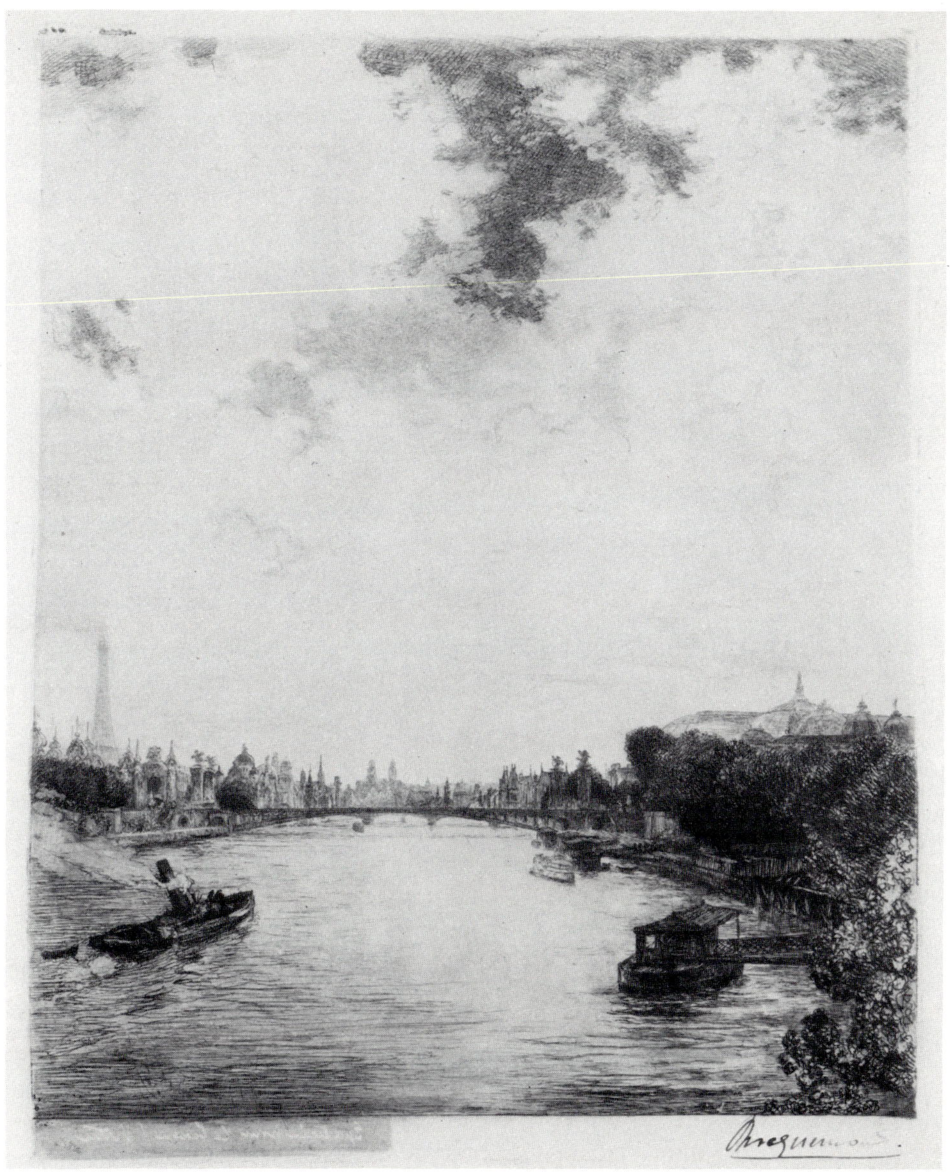

Maxime Lalanne.

14 *Bordeaux*.

Etching, 1866.
8-5/16 x 11-13/16 inches (21.1 x 30 cm.).
Béraldi number 10. Gift of Mr. Ralph King. CMA 20.692

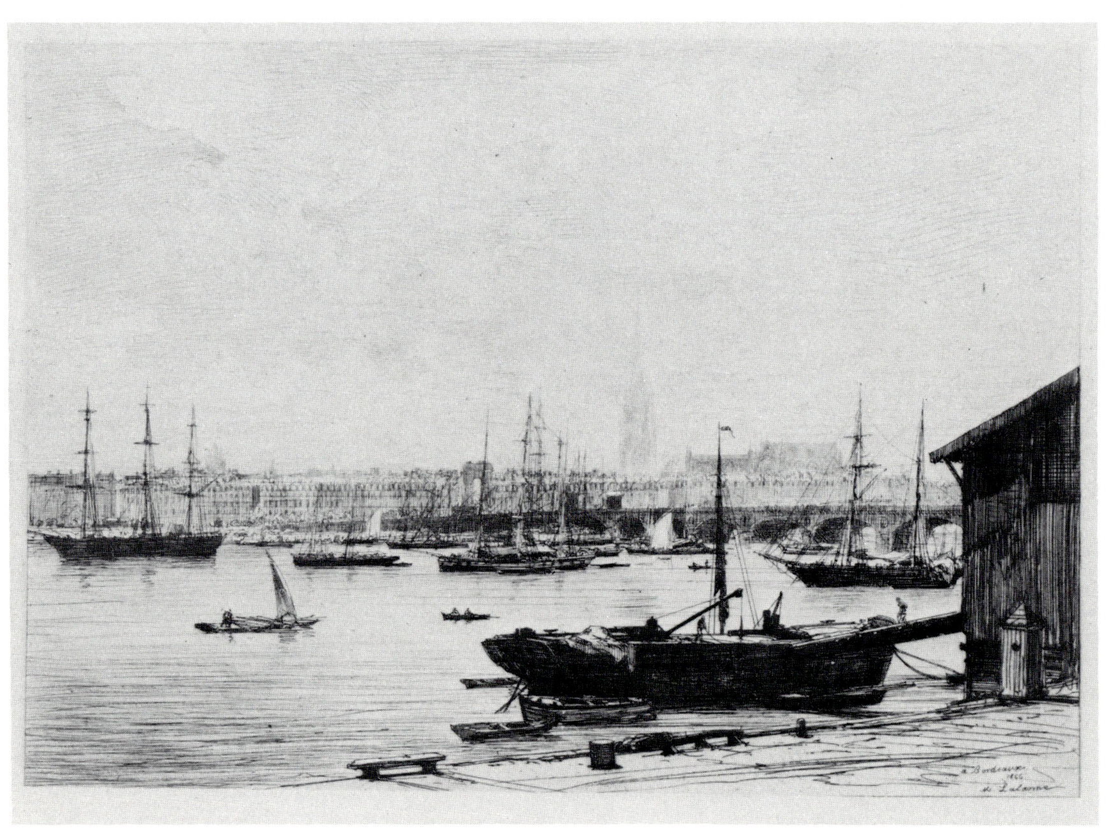

Frank Duveneck, American, 1848-1919.

15 *Laguna, Venice.*
Etching, ca. 1880.
7-7/8 x 13-1/2 inches (20 x 34.3 cm.).
Cincinnati Art Museum number 110. Gift of Mr. Ralph King. CMA 23.1114

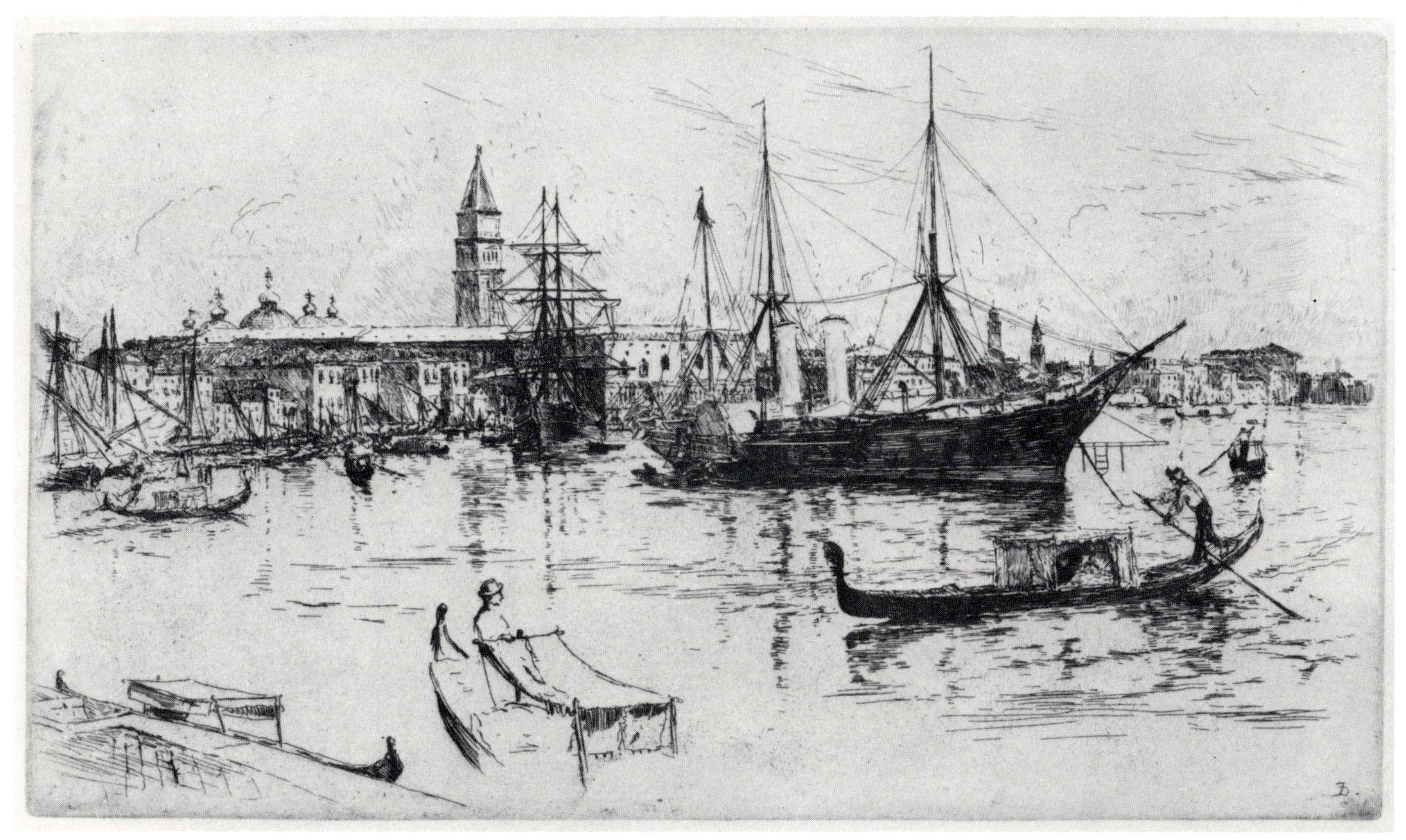

Frank Duveneck.

16 *San Trovasso Canal, Venice.*
Etching, 1883.
7-3/4 x 19-1/2 inches (19.7 x 49.5 cm.).
Cincinnati Art Museum number 131. Gift of The Cincinnati Art Museum. CMA 33.71

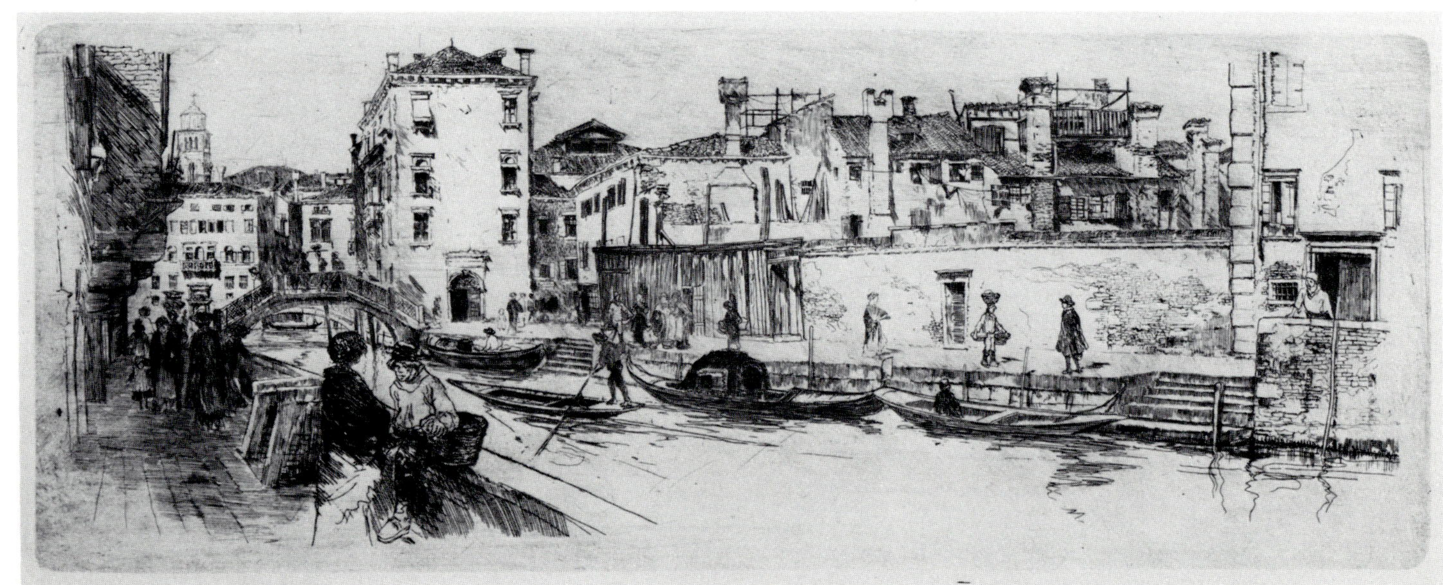

John Marin,
American, 1870-1953.

17 *From Ponte S. Pantaleo, Venice.*

Etching, 1907.
7-7/8 x 5-1/2 inches
(20 x 14 cm.).
Zigrosser number 58.
Lent by Associated
American Artists,
New York.

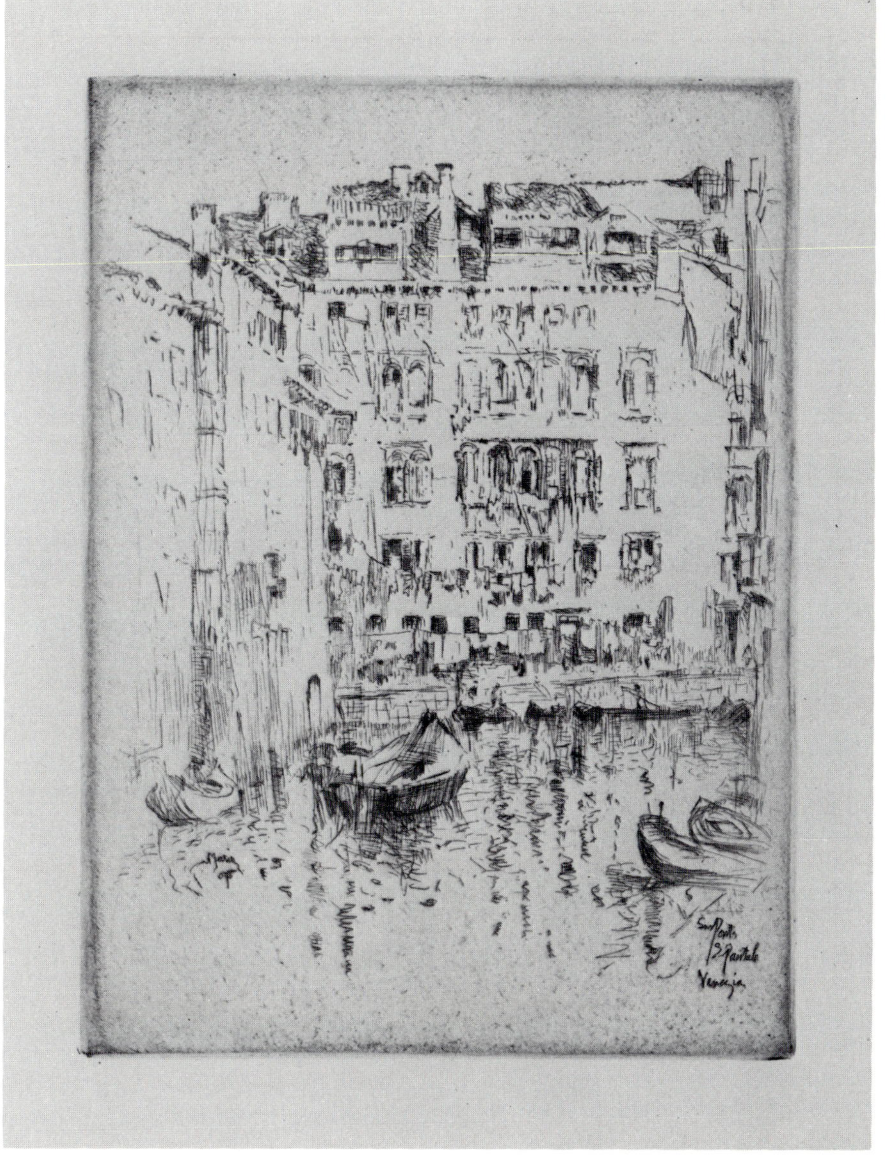

Joseph Pennell, American, 1860-1926.

18 *East Bank of the Schuylkill Looking North.*
Etching, 1881. 7-1/2 x 9-3/4 inches (19 x 24.8 cm.).
Wuerth number 31. Gift of Mr. and Mrs. Allen T. Frary. CMA 66.101

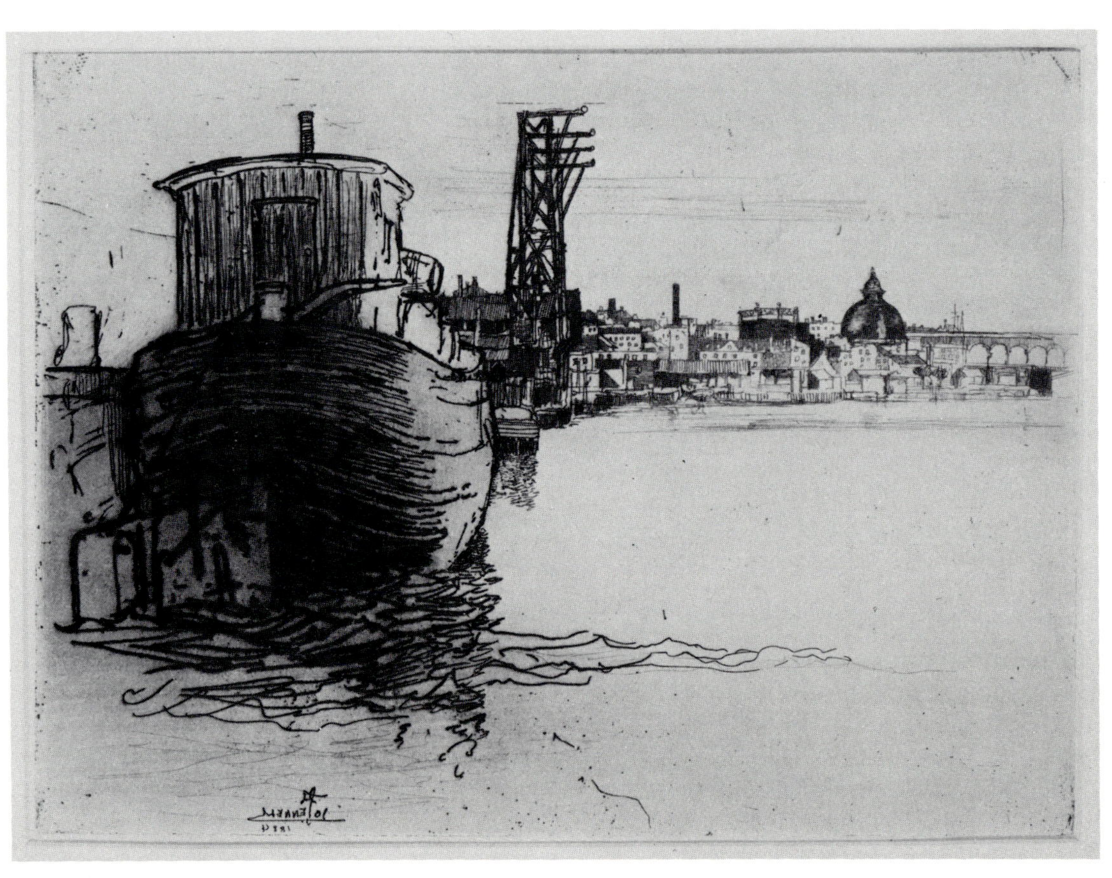

Joseph Pennell.

19 *Wren's City.*

Mezzotint, 1909. 10 x 11-7/8 inches (25.4 x 30.2 cm.).
Wuerth number 504. Lent by Associated American Artists, New York.

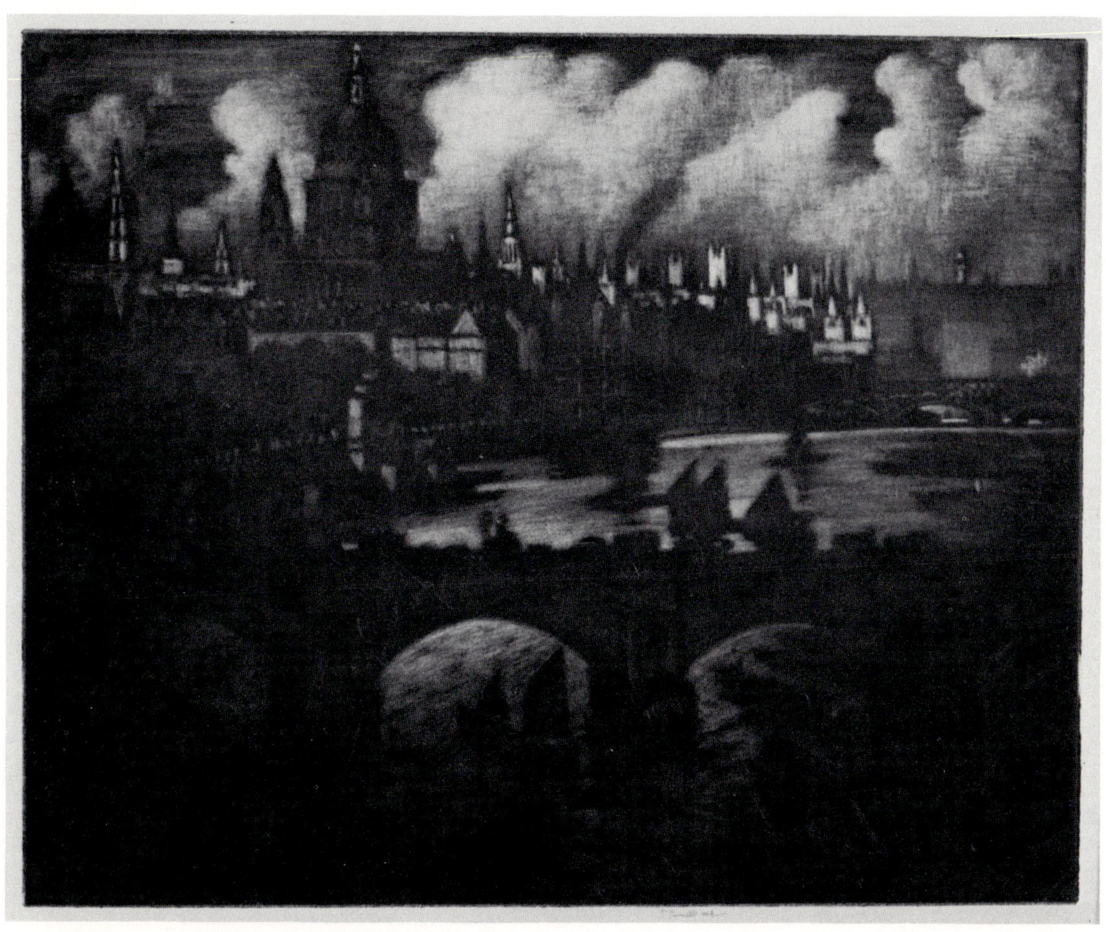

I. ENVIRONMENT: RURAL AND CITY

C. Cityscape

During the course of the nineteenth century, the face of many cities began to change. Spurred on by the desire to modernize the environment under the guise of beautification programs, architects urged the dismantling of old buildings in order to create wide vistas fit for modern traffic. Roads were paved, monuments from the past often destroyed, creating a sense of dislocation and frustration among the inhabitants of a given city. In place of old tenements, architects devised a network of modern buildings which climbed higher than before, rivaling the medieval cathedrals in the prominence they acquired. The skyscraper quickly became the icon of the late nineteenth century. Without past styles to haunt them and the problems of clearing away centuries of old buildings as found in Paris, America became the new republic where the art form of the twentieth century—the gigantic architectural structure—was recorded. The inhabitants of the city were soon dwarfed not by mountains but by buildings of cement and steel which created small canyons in which the people of a city could move.

The first phase of the dehumanization of the city was found during the 1860's when Paris was torn apart in order to create wide vistas for the Second Empire. Old tenements were destroyed as street improvements—under the banner of progress—were recorded by Maxime Lalanne in his *Démolitions pour le Percement du Boulevard St. Germain* [20]. By the latter part of the century and the turn of the next, attention had shifted from Paris toward recording contemporary architecture in other cities. Buildings had been constructed, and America revealed a penchant for the urban environment which limited the presence of trees, replacing them with macadam streets and stone buildings [21]. Everywhere print-makers looked, the city was defined by tall structures, against which light played as on an ancient ruin. *The Stock Exchange, Philadelphia* by Joseph Pennell [22] or *The Woolworth, Through the Arch* [23] were the new sights framed by the printmaker, symbolizing the enthusiasm of new forms.

When John Taylor Arms recorded facades, as in *An American Cathedral* [24], he framed the shapes through vistas created by other monuments and demonstrated how the skyscraper dwarfed inhabitants and New York's City Hall alike. During the 1930's, Arms expanded his documentation of New York by observing the rapid growth of many buildings from the window of an art dealer—Knoedler. He was careful to juxtapose the office buildings with their small counterparts below in an effort to arrange the shapes as a still-life artist might organize his forms. The air was still and the presence of inhabitants was eliminated from view [25].

Continually drawn to other locales through his constant trips abroad, Arms saw Gerona, Spain [26] as an older example of the problems found in modern city life. The crowding of the buildings and the mounting of forms one on top of the other was being repeated in America where the lessons of Europe were not being observed. Even on visits to Stockholm [27] Arms meticulously revealed his penchant for an architectural setting devoid of human beings—demonstrating that cities throughout the world were becoming impersonal locales attractive to artists for the combination of shapes and textures but likely to raise serious problems for those who inhabited its tightly controlled space. Similarly, a personal view of New York such as Arms's *Out of My Window* [28] reiterates the theme of city living where edifices tower above older tenements.

Maxime Lalanne.

20 *Demolitions for the Opening of the Boulevard St. Germain*
(Démolitions pour le Percement du Boulevard St.-Germain).
Etching, 1862. 8-3/8 x 12-1/8 inches (21.3 x 30.8 cm.).
Béraldi number 4. Gift of Frederick Keppel and Co., Inc. CMA 18.101

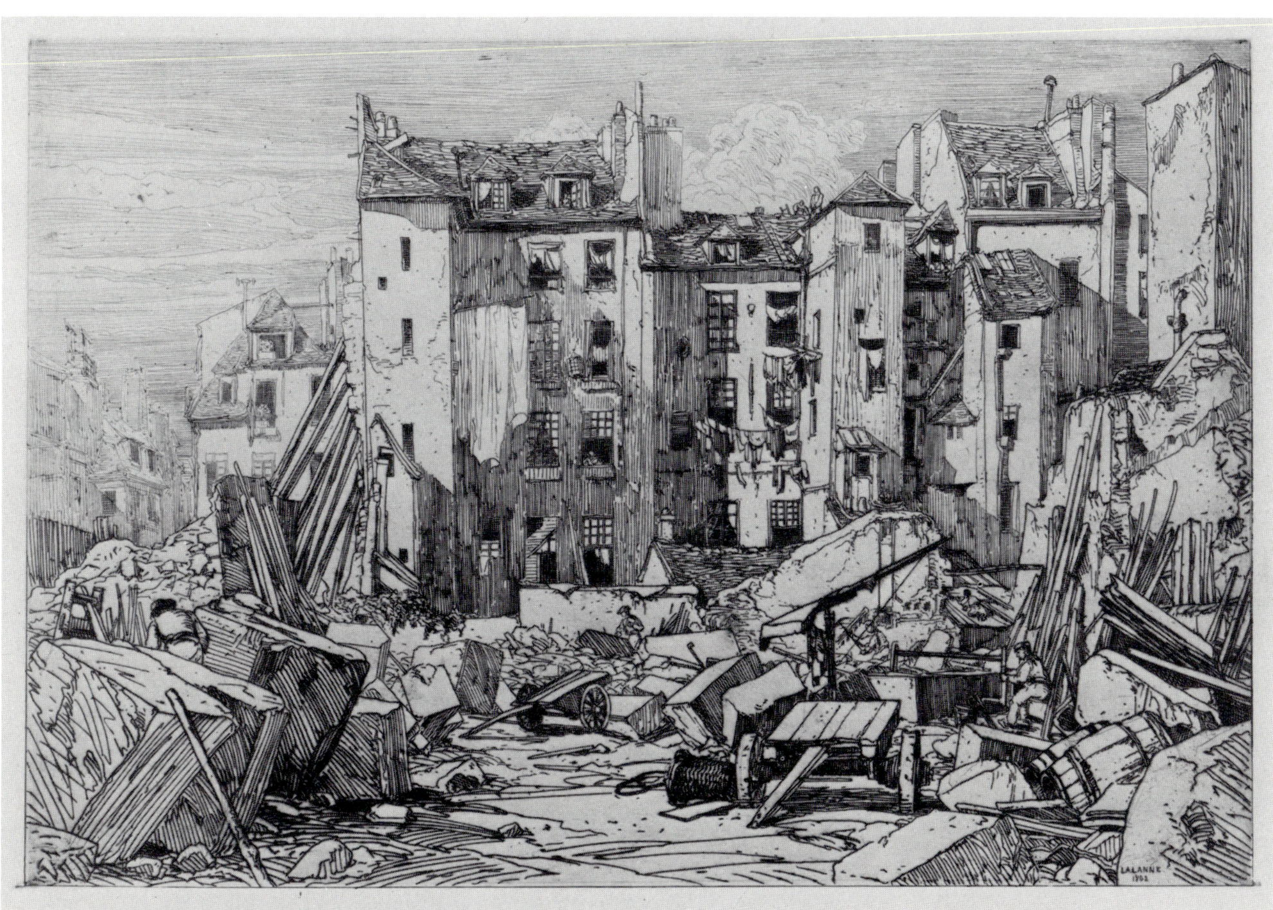

Joseph Pennell.

21 *Ferry House,
from Pierrepont Street.*
Etching, 1924.
10 x 7-7/8 inches
(25.4 x 20 cm.).
Wuerth number 833.
Lent by Associated
American Artists,
New York.

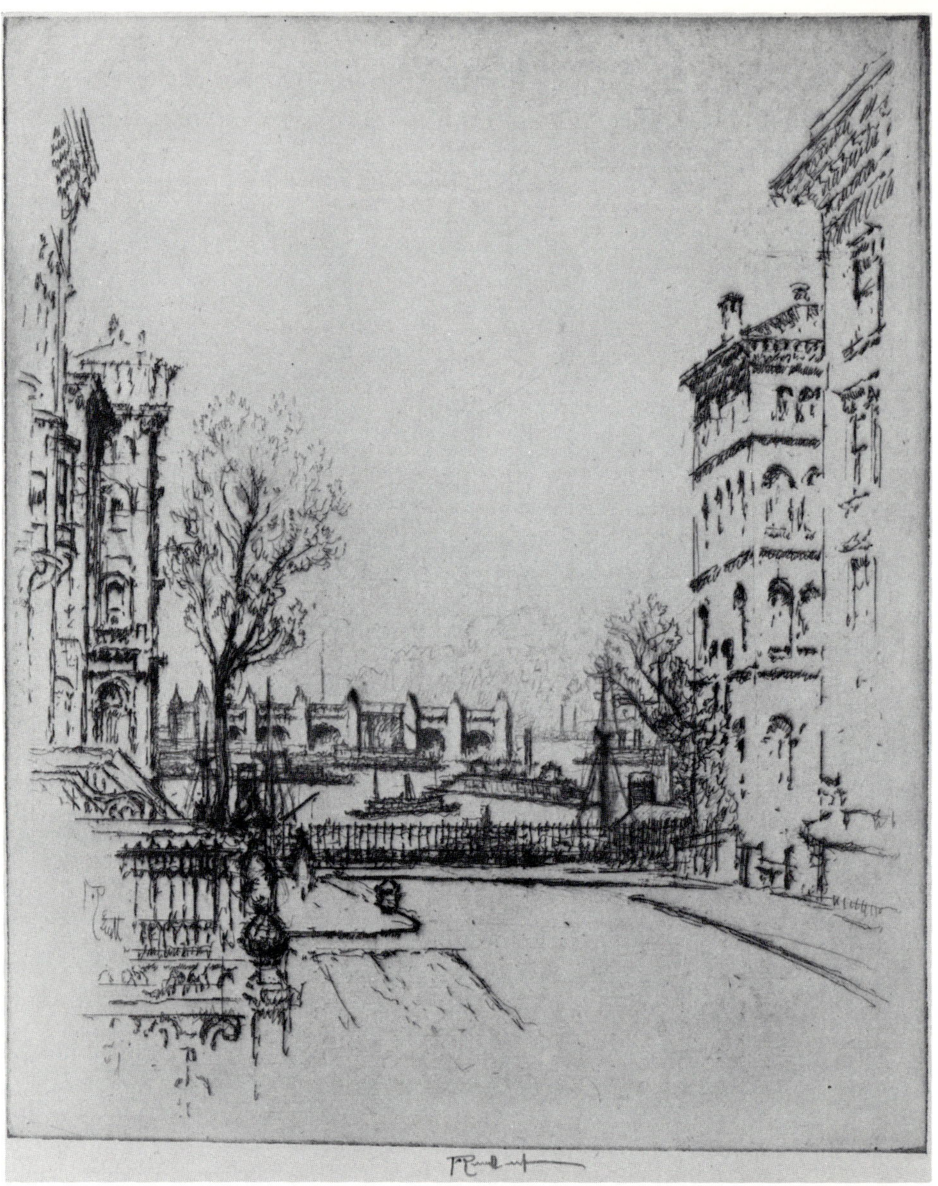

Joseph Pennell.

22 *Stock Exchange,
Philadelphia.*
Etching, 1920.
9-1/2 x 7-3/4 inches
(24.1 x 19.7 cm.).
Wuerth number 741.
Lent by Associated
American Artists,
New York.

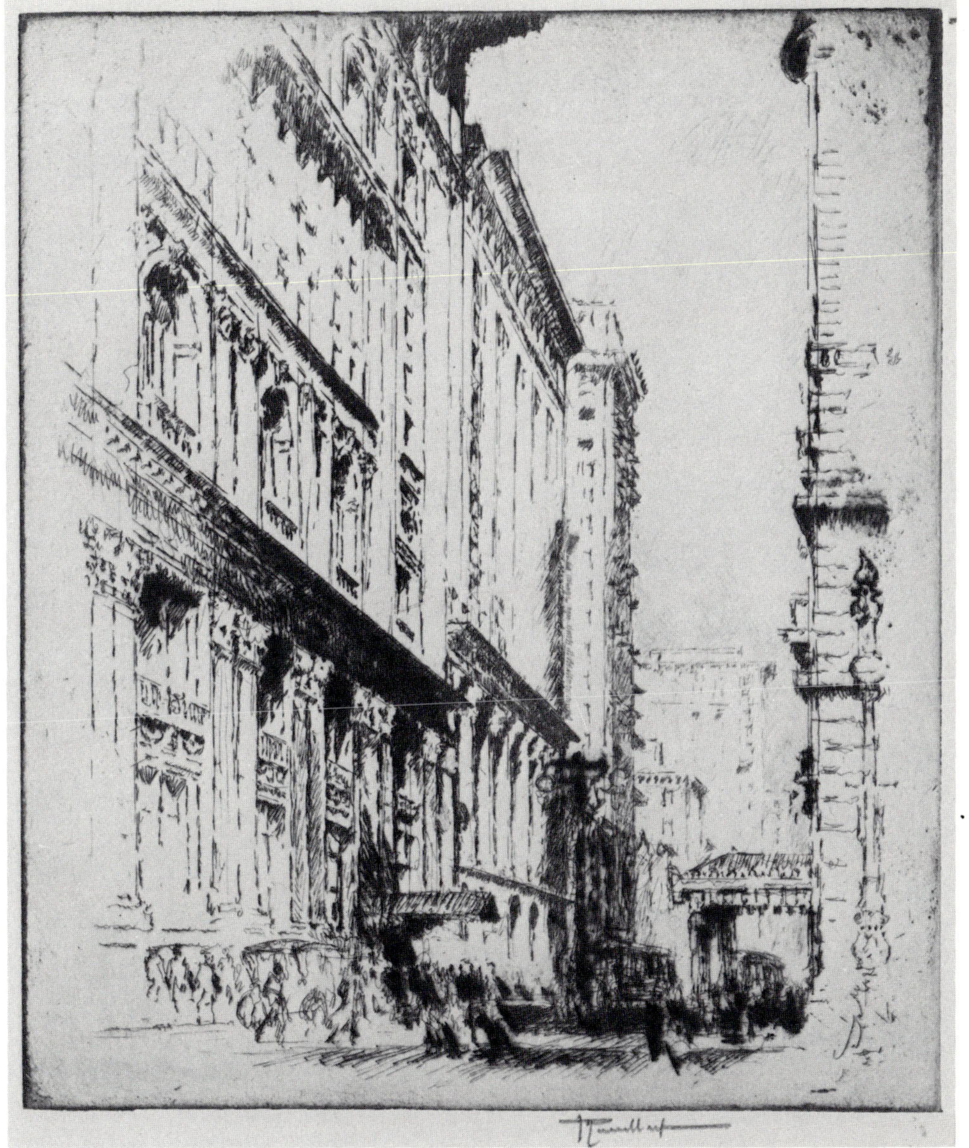

Joseph Pennell.

23 *The Woolworth, Through the Arch.*
Etching, 1921.
9-7/8 x 6-7/8 inches
(25.1 x 17.5 cm.).
Wuerth number 785.
Lent by Associated
American Artists,
New York.

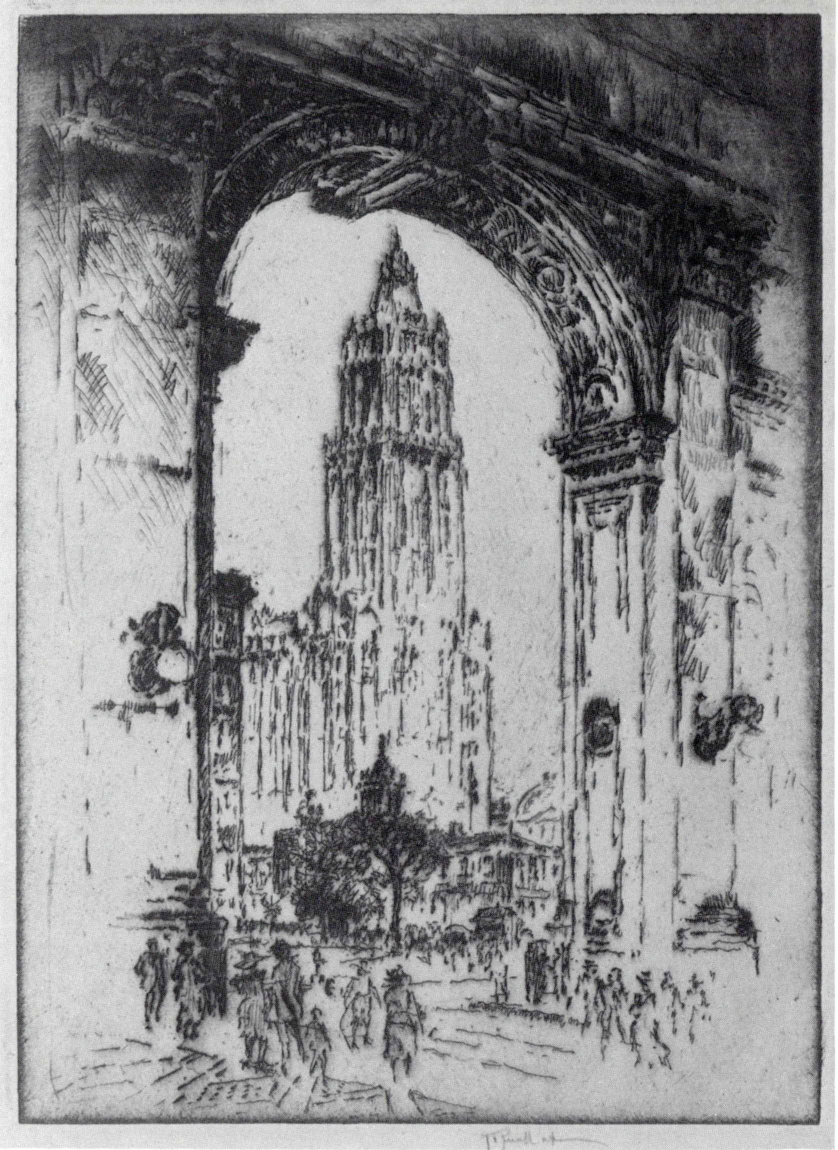

John Taylor Arms.

24 *An American Cathedral.*
Etching, 1921.
17-1/4 x 6-3/4 inches
(43.8 x 17.2 cm.).
American Etchers,
Volume V, number 67.
Lent by Associated
American Artists,
New York.

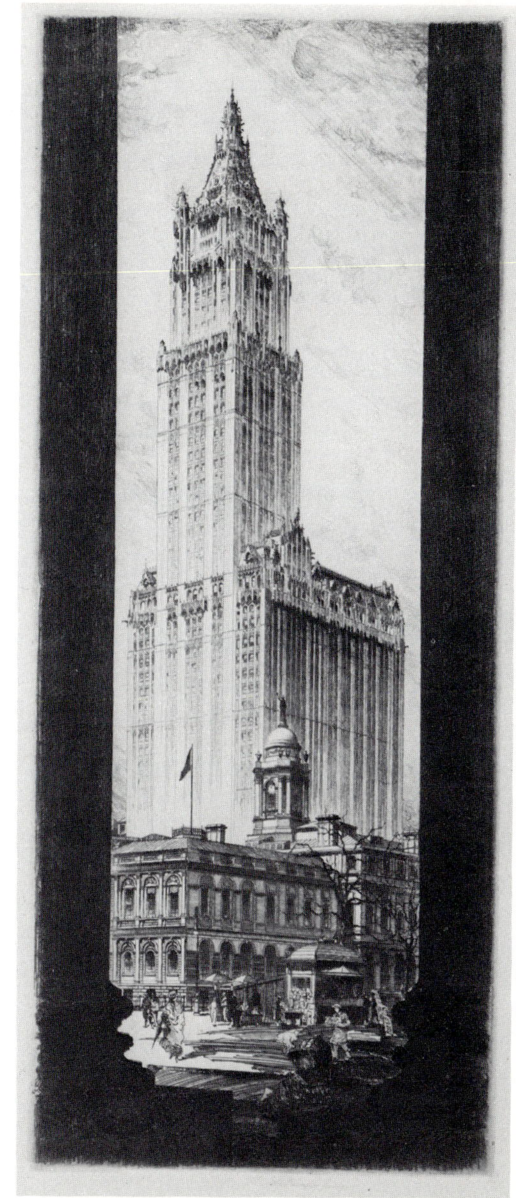

John Taylor Arms.

25 *From Knoedler's Window, MCMXXXV.*
Etching, 1935. 4-15/16 x 5-1/16 inches (12.6 x 12.8 cm.).
New York Public Library number 297.
Gift of Henry S. Francis. CMA 66.90

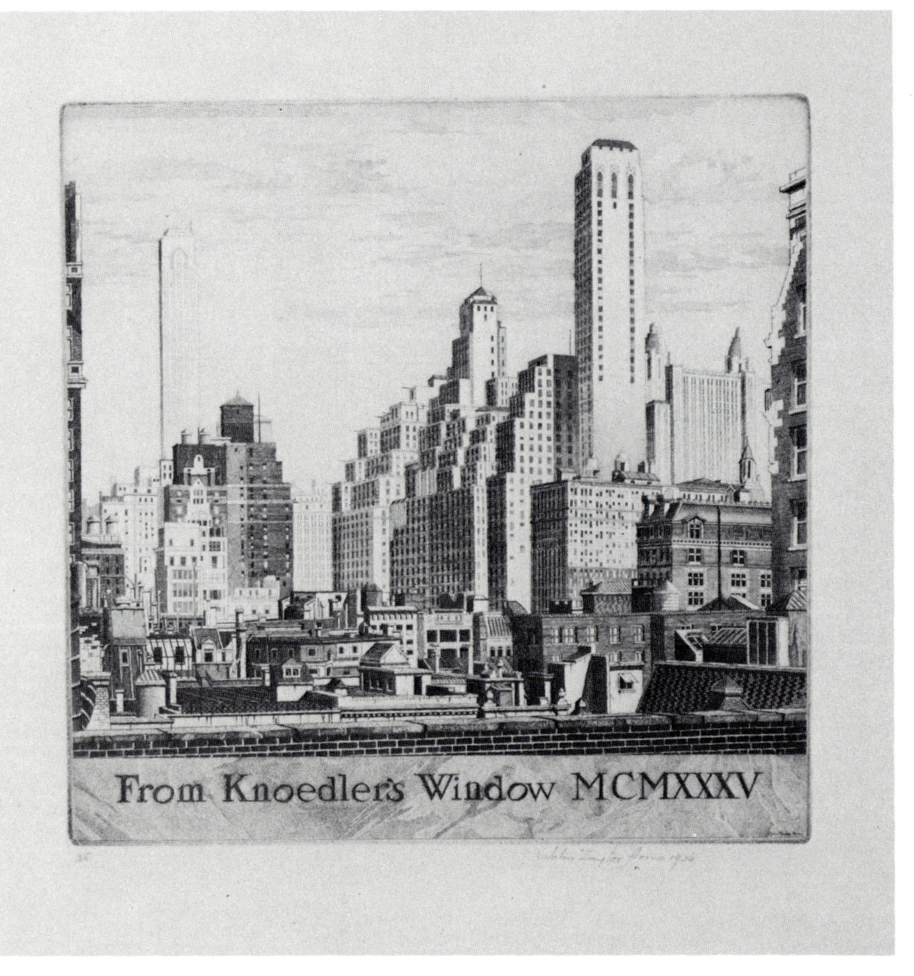

John Taylor Arms.

26 *Gerona, Spain.*
Etching, 1925.
12-1/4 x 7-3/4 inches
(31.1 x 19.7 cm.).
New York Public
Library number 166.
Lent by Associated
American Artists,
New York.

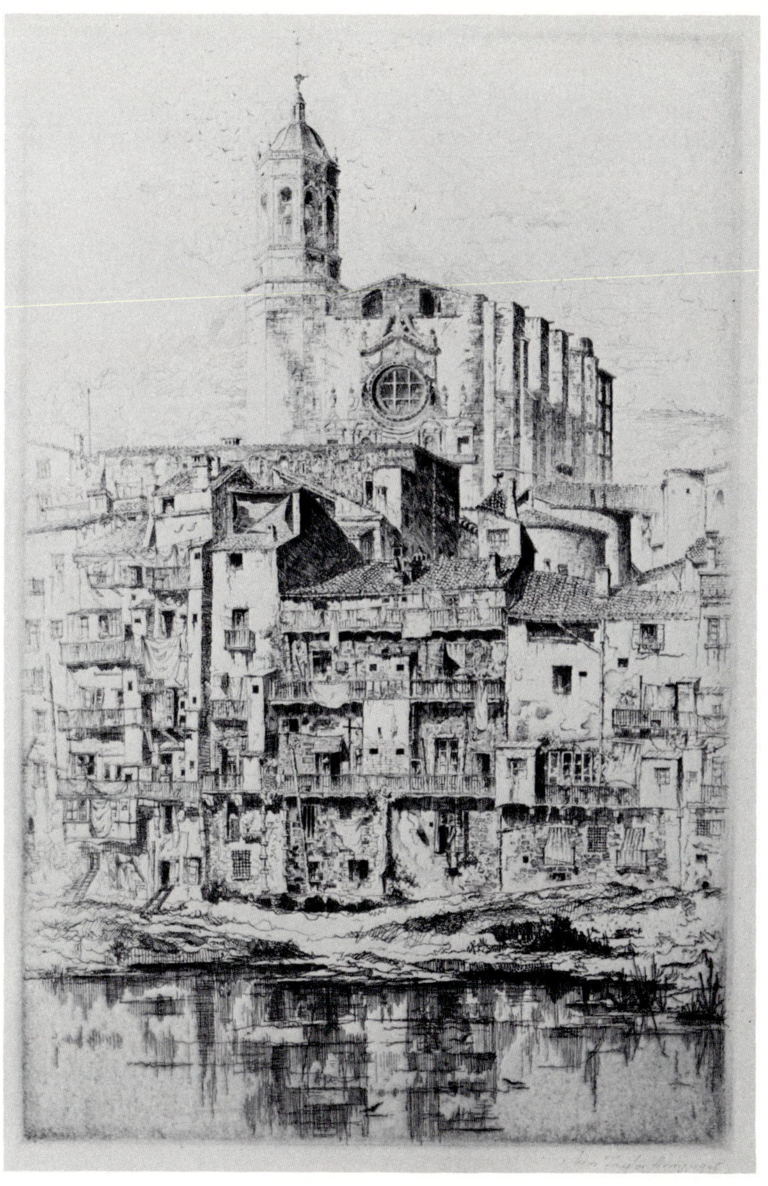

John Taylor Arms.

27 *Stockholm.*

Etching, 1940. 7-7/8 x 13-1/2 inches (20 x 34.3 cm.).
Kennedy Galleries number 78. Lent by Associated American Artists, New York.

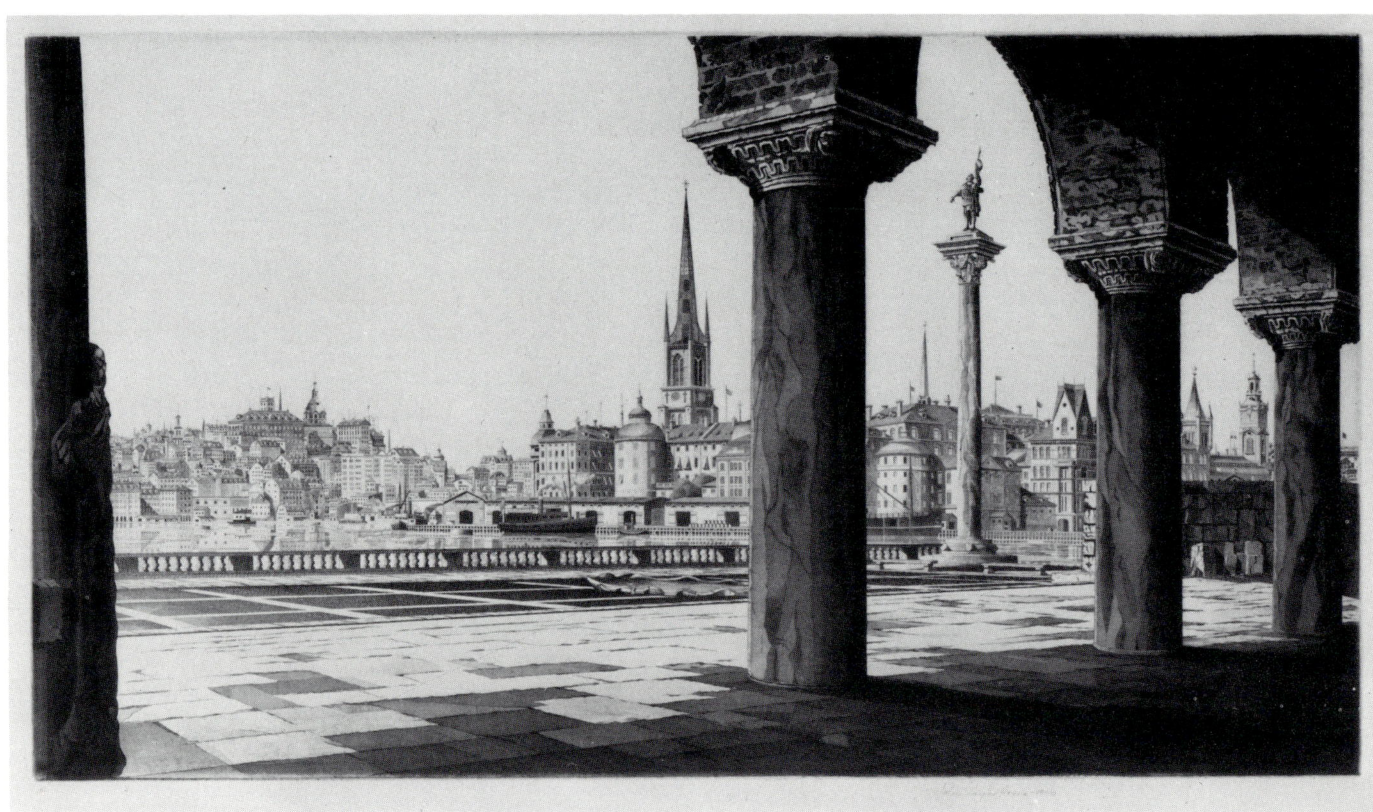

John Taylor Arms.
28 *Out of My Window.*
Etching, 1916.
7-9/16 x 5-9/16 inches
(19.2 x 14.2 cm.).
American Etchers,
Volume V, number 4.
Lent by Associated
American Artists,
New York.

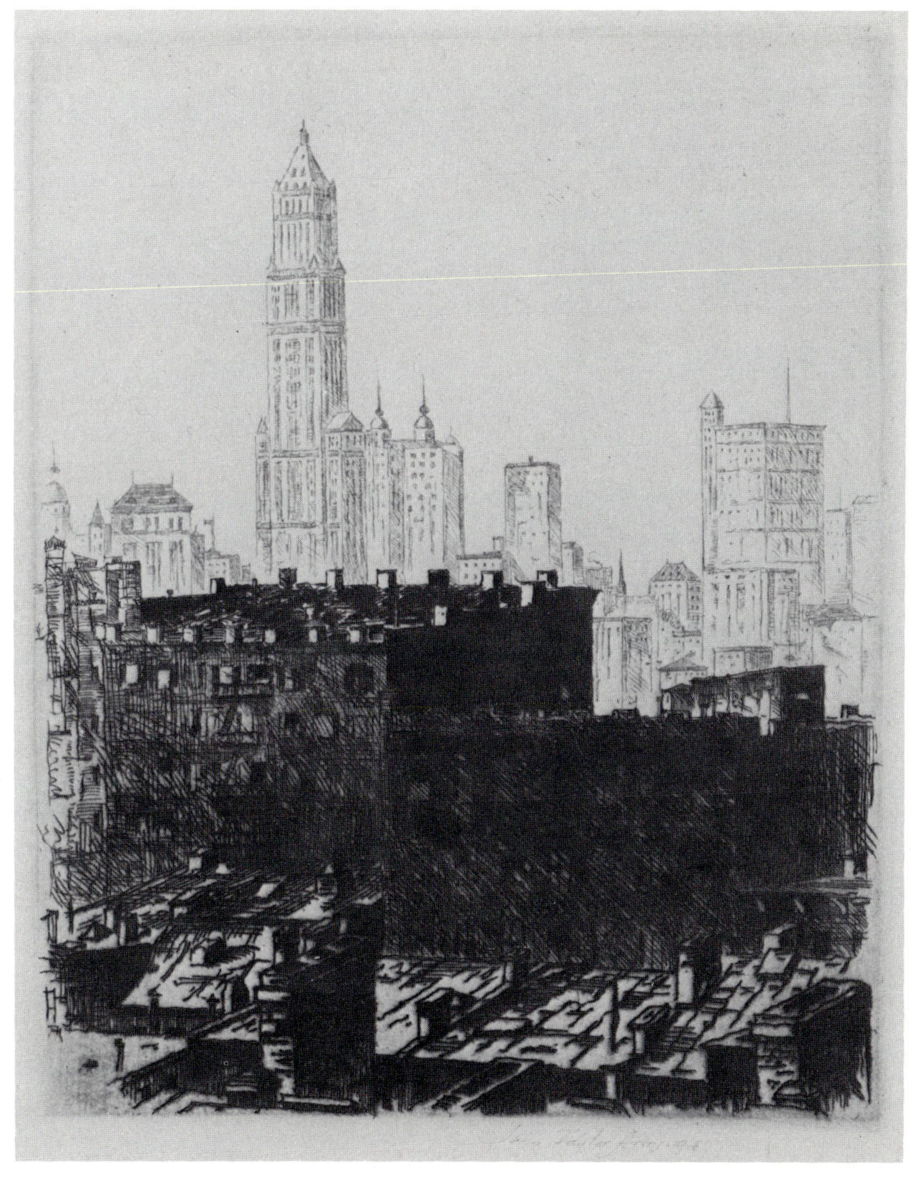

II. ENVIRONMENT: PAST AND PRESENT

A. Romantic Monuments

As changes in city planning led to the desecration of old monuments and paved broad avenues replaced the small pathways of medieval Paris, artists saw their fond past being destroyed. As part of the Gothic revival tendency, preservation movements emerged in France and England to prevent the destruction of medieval buildings. Printmakers also reacted by turning a romantic eye toward remnants of the past which had survived centuries of neglect. They selected monuments with a past tradition and sought to glorify these ancient remnants with the romantic cloak of heroism and majesty. Notre-Dame, and other architectural monuments like it, became symbols of the past surviving into the present—guiding beacons of the value artists placed on the preservation of older values in an age given to commercialism.

Charles Meryon emerged as one of the foremost printmakers absorbed by the romantic appreciation of medieval cathedrals. His etching of *La Galerie Notre-Dame, Paris* [29] not only reveals a meticulous study of architectural detail—Meryon had a preservationist's spirit but also evokes a sense of brooding mystery appropriate to a romantic interpretation of the past. Similarly, *Le Stryge* [30] singles out one architectural form, a gargoyle from Notre-Dame's facade, to emphasize the changing face of Paris.

The stately appreciation of cathedrals was maintained by D.Y. Cameron (1865-1945) who visited France as a traveller. His view of *Saint Germain l'Auxerrois* [31] or *Beaufort's Tower, St. Cross* [32] shows how sensitively did printmakers study passages of light across a stationary surface. Undoubtedly their interest was conditioned by the theory of the picturesque—which advocated awareness of architectural monuments—and which had been revived during the latter part of the nineteenth century by artists who refused to accept "progress" as the only cry of the age. Once again, as in the eighteenth century, the architecture of the past became a source of appreciation and intense study. The cult of ruins was now bolstered by a fully developed romantic atmosphere which venerated these old monuments.

As the century changed, John Taylor Arms continued this tradition. His images from the 1920's—of gargoyles perched and straining to see the city below—were highly suggestive of his understanding of prints by Meryon. Yet, he emphasized the grotesqueness of their shapes—almost as if in an architectural detail he was trying to find some primeval strength which could counteract the mechanized world of the twentieth century. Arms' prints reacquaint one with brutish, almost primitive, sensations which he tried to symbolize through the romantic fondness for the Gothic. It is a curious recurrence of this revival quality in the midst of an age pursuing other ends [33, 34]. Arms, by 1930, did not lessen his examination of architecture—witness his *Gothic Glory, Sens* [35] where he found consolation for the drab environment in a meticulous study of the facade's tracery.

With the full flowering of Arms' study of medieval architecture, the appreciation of past monuments had lasted almost a century. New shapes—the skyscraper—dominated the city. Some printmakers such as Cameron and Arms advocated, through their selection of theme, a humane study of the past, providing them with moments of majestic contemplation at a time when they were alienated from their own modern environment.

Charles Meryon.

29 *La Galerie Notre-Dame, Paris.*
Etching, 1853.
11-1/8 x 6-15/16 inches
(28.3 x 17.7 cm.).
Delteil and Wright
number 26, iii.
Bequest of Grover
Higgins. CMA 53.682

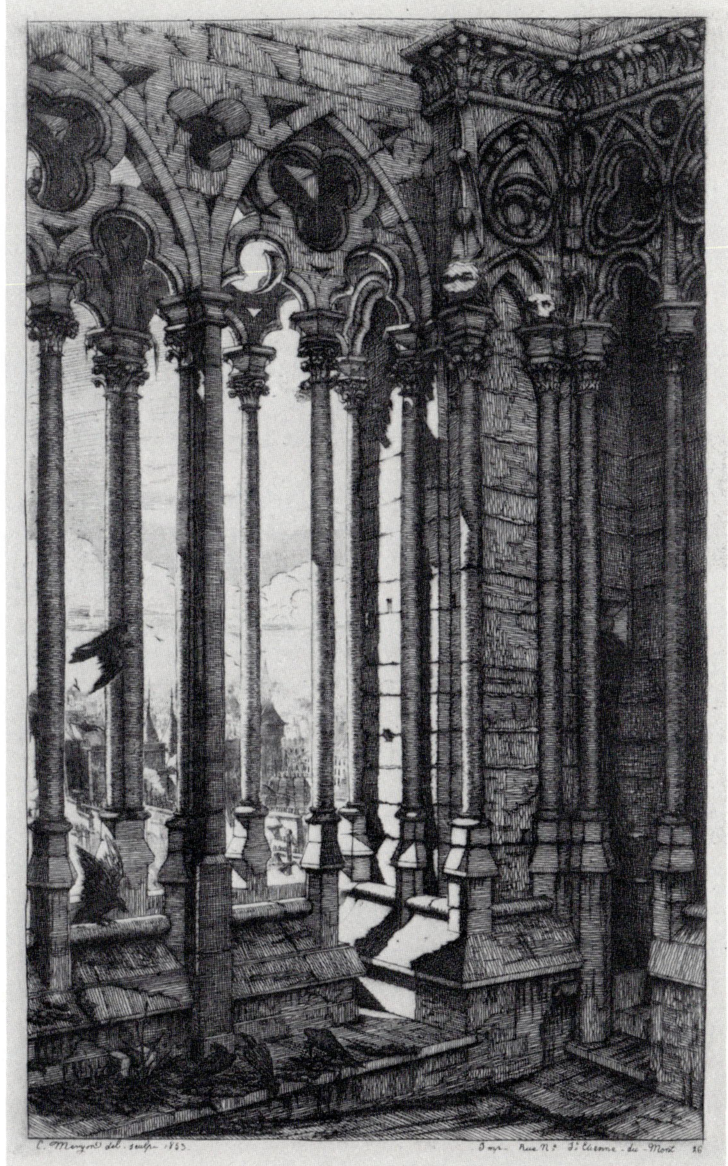

Charles Meryon.

30 *The Vampire (Le Stryge).*
Etching, 1853.
6-5/8 x 5-1/16 inches
(16.8 x 12.8 cm.).
Delteil and Wright
number 23, iv.
Gift of Grover
Higgins. CMA 41.298

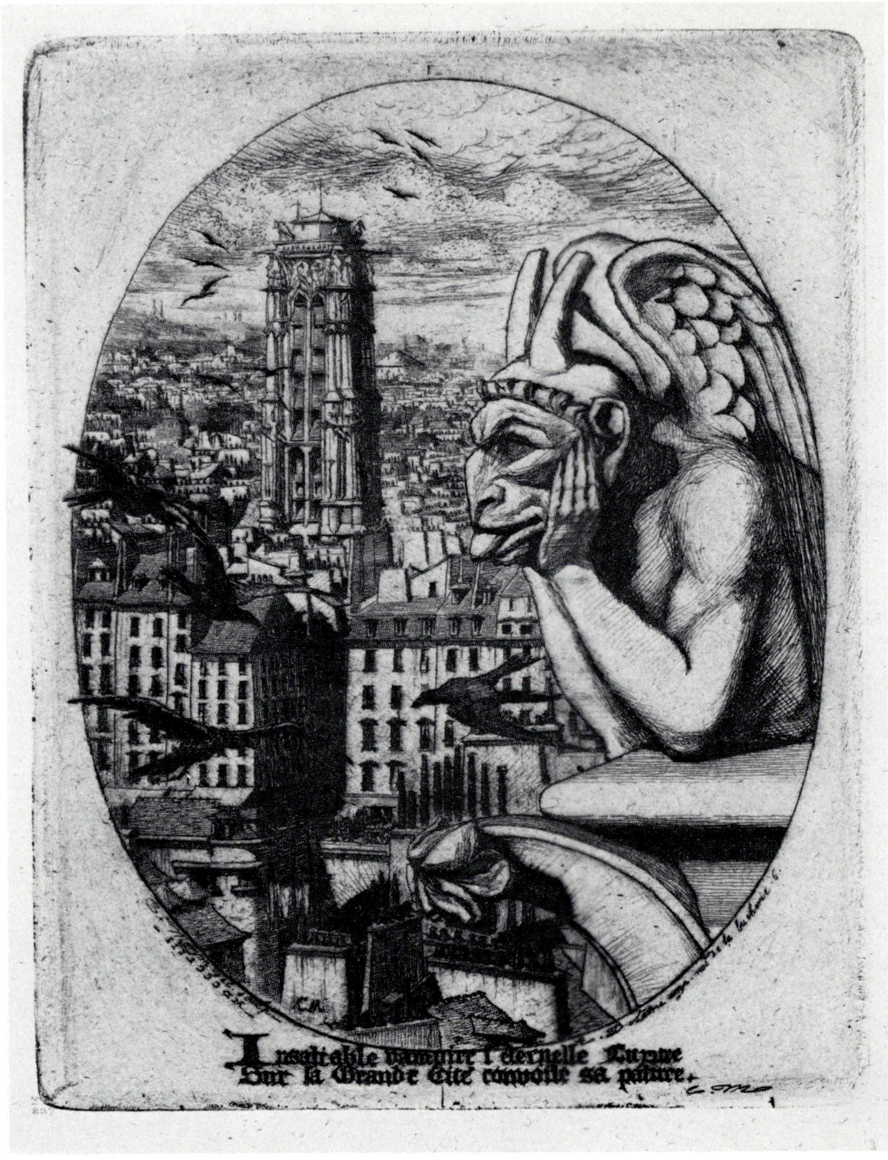

D. Y. Cameron.

31 *Saint Germain at Auxerrois
(Saint Germain l'Auxerrois).*
Etching and Drypoint, 1904.
12-15/32 x 6-13/32 inches
(31.6 x 16.3 cm.).
Rinder number 362.
Lent by The College
of Wooster.

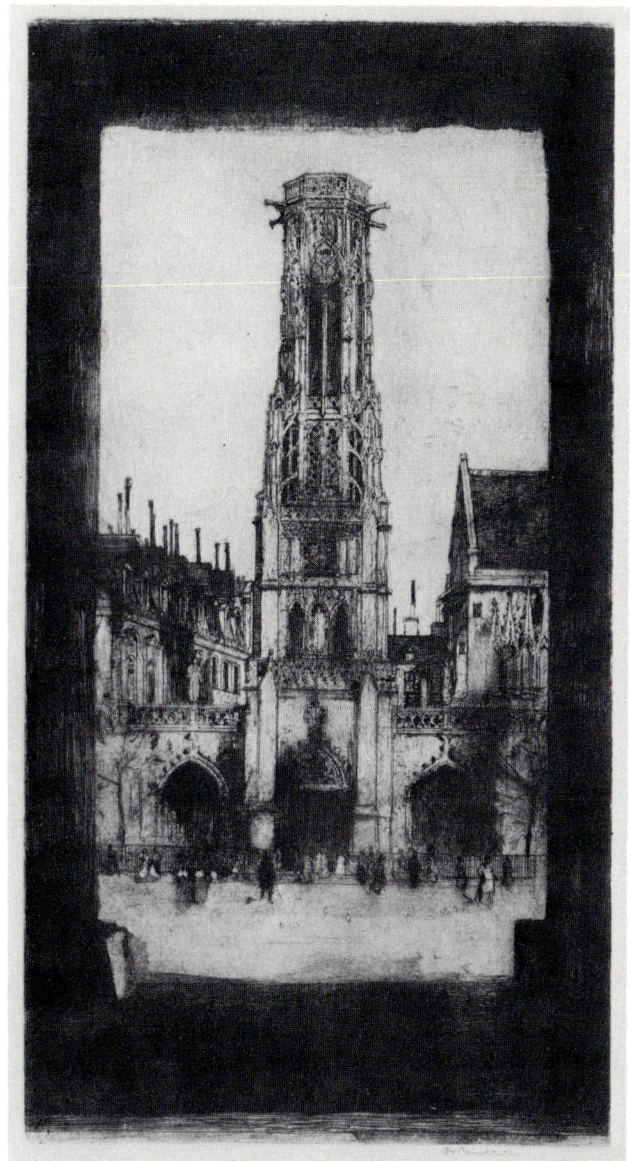

D. Y. Cameron.

32 *Beaufort's Tower,
St. Cross.*

Etching, 1902.
5-25/32 x 3-23/32 inches
(14.7 x 9.6 cm.).
Rinder number 342.
Lent by The College
of Wooster.

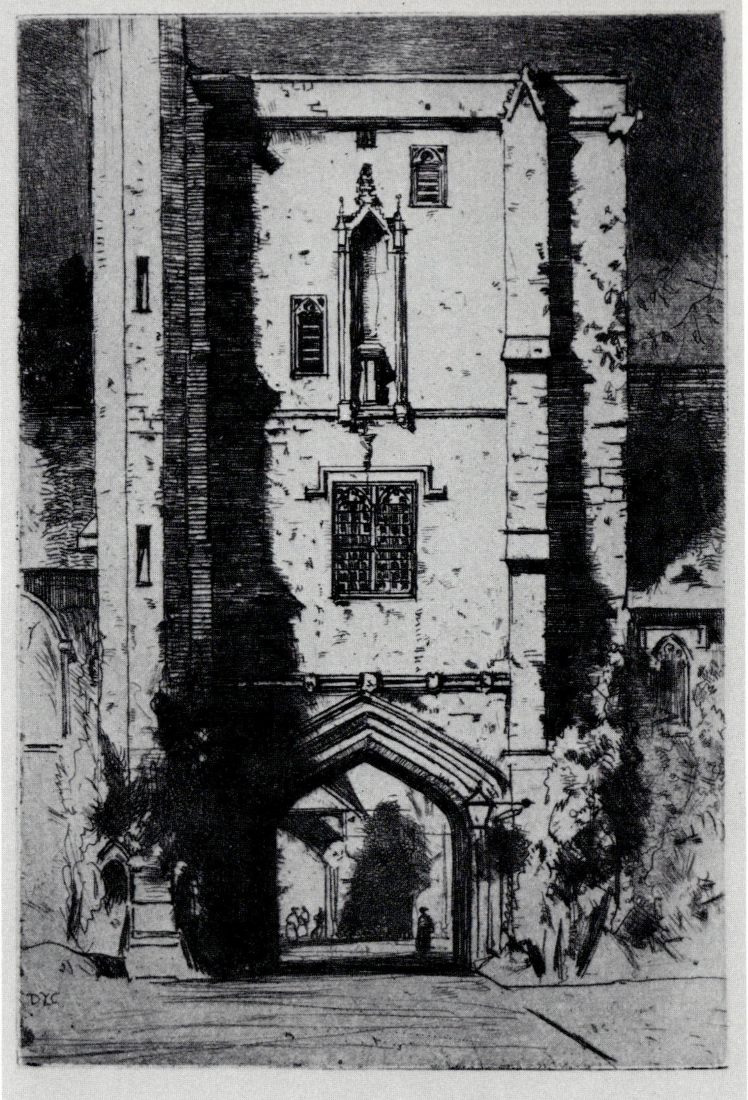

John Taylor Arms.

33 *Watching the People Below, Amiens.*
Etching, 1921. 4-7/8 x 8-1/8 inches (12.4 x 20.6 cm.).
American Etchers, Volume V, number 62. Lent by Associated American Artists, New York.

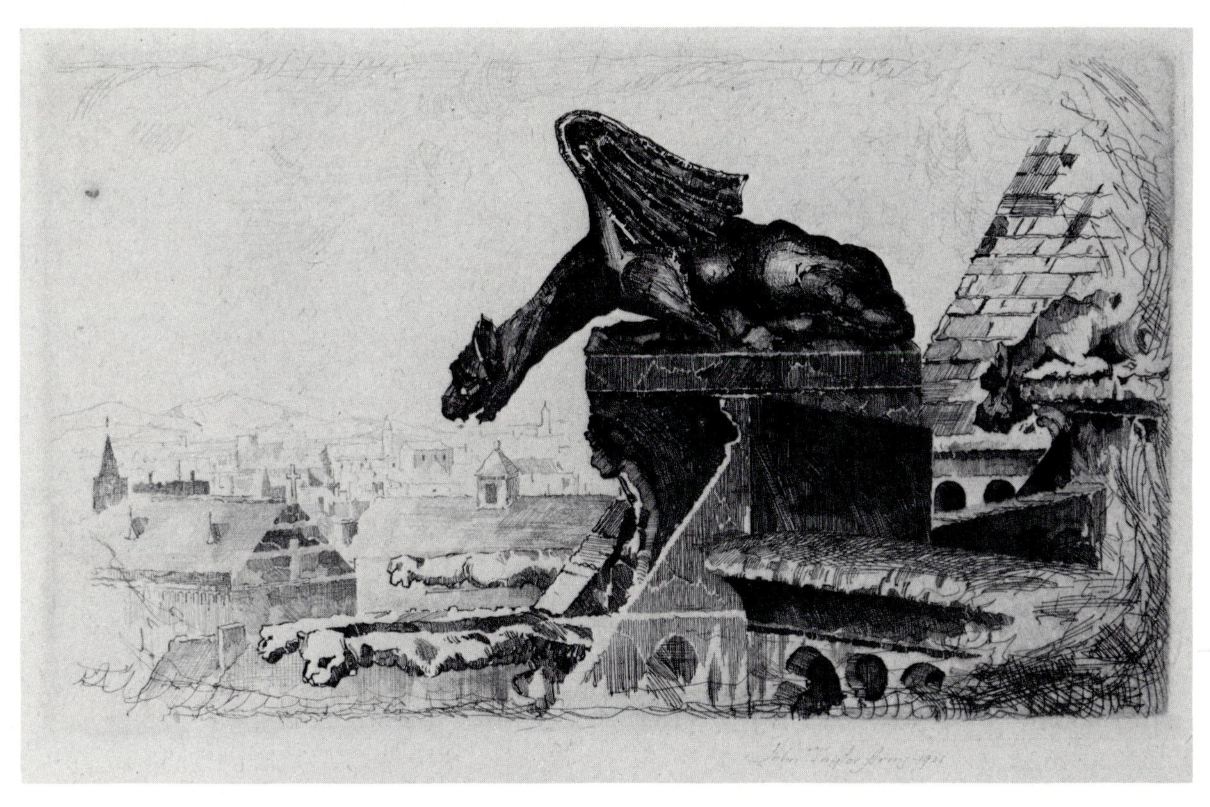

John Taylor Arms.

34 *A Chimera.*

Etching, 1948.
2-7/8 x 2-3/8 inches (7.3 x 6 cm.).
New York Public Library number 419a.
Lent by Associated American Artists,
New York.

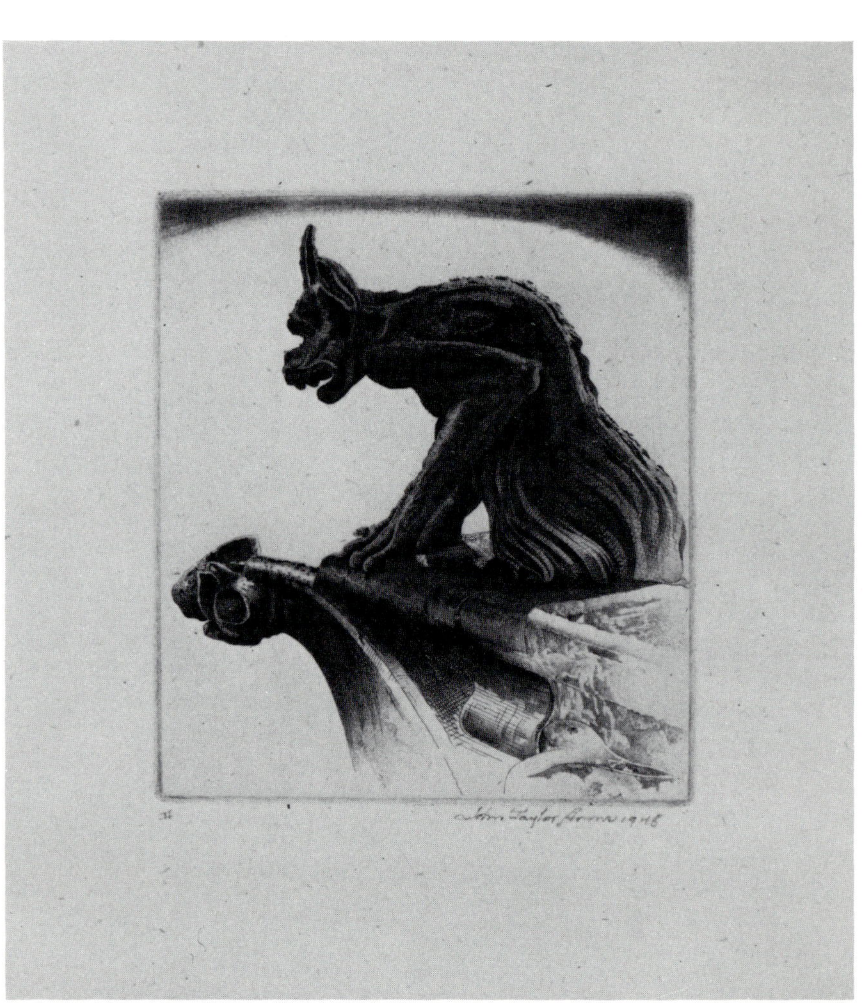

John Taylor Arms.

35 *Gothic Glory, Sens.*
Etching, 1929.
15-3/16 x 9-1/8 inches
(38.6 x 23.2 cm.).
American Etchers,
Volume V, number 142.
Lent by Associated
American Artists,
New York.

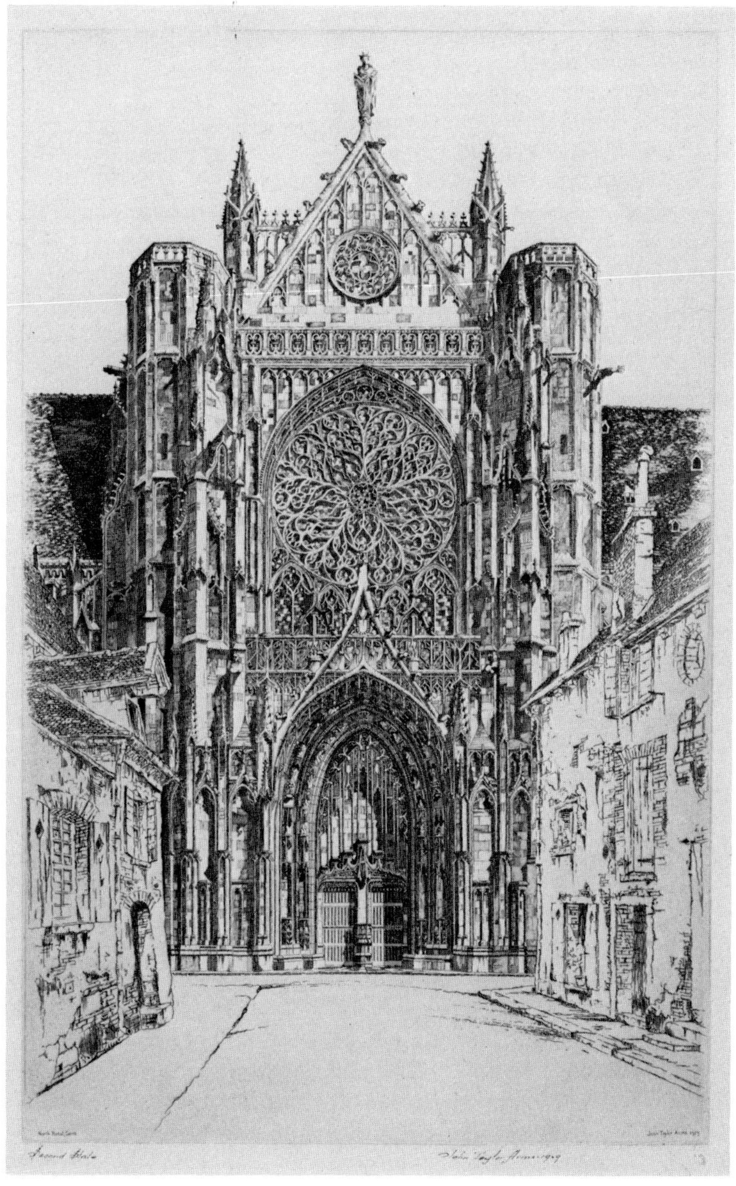

II. ENVIRONMENT: PAST AND PRESENT

B. Picturesque Views

Printmakers also devoted considerable attention to the dwellings of the common man, recording dilapidated and rustic settings which evoked sympathy. Often overwhelmed by cathedrals or skyscrapers, artists tried to find how ordinary houses survived as a means of relating to the lower classes. The tenements of the nineteenth century gradually became the picturesque sights of the twentieth century as travellers to rural locations were intrigued by locales they thought no longer existed.

James McNeill Whistler (1834-1903) was among those printmakers attracted to the slums of mid-century. Frequently appalled by social conditions which were unsanitary and unhealthy, Whistler demonstrated in his *The Unsafe Tenement* [36] just what a deplorable atmosphere some people lived in. Social reformers tried to improve the quality of life during the latter part of the nineteenth century, but unfortunately tenement crowding could not be alleviated in Europe or the United States. To Whistler's contemporary, Maxime Lalanne, the small village—with rustic shops and quaint alleyways—became a novel way for artists to picture a provincial locale. By seeing villages outside Paris [37] as reminders of a simple existence, artists further transformed the qualities of innocence extolled in nature into an idiom of escape.

Again, John Taylor Arms became the spokesman—through his prints—of the return toward more humble settings evoking earlier times. Whether the village was Rouen [38] or simply old houses in the Rue Dacier [39], Arms singled out dwellings and streets that had a long history [40, 41]. His frequent travels to Europe led him to forgotten pathways where the cycle of life remained unchanged for centuries, and where the houses of the common people were huddled together as if for protection.

Arms' evocation of secluded locales and untrodden paths spread to his examination of America's past. Eager to escape into the calm of nature, Arms found an old cabin [42] or a sturdy mill [43] as reminders of the pioneering spirit. He helped transfer an interest in old dwellings to a new locale—America—in the hope that the values of preserving the past would not eliminate the picturesque rustic setting from the vocabulary of an artist sensitively attuned to the isolation of modern life.

James Abbott McNeill Whistler, American, 1834-1903.

36 *The Unsafe Tenement.*

Etching, undated. 6-1/8 x 8-3/4 inches (15.5 x 22.2 cm.).
Kennedy number 17, ii. Bequest of James Parmelee. CMA 40.802

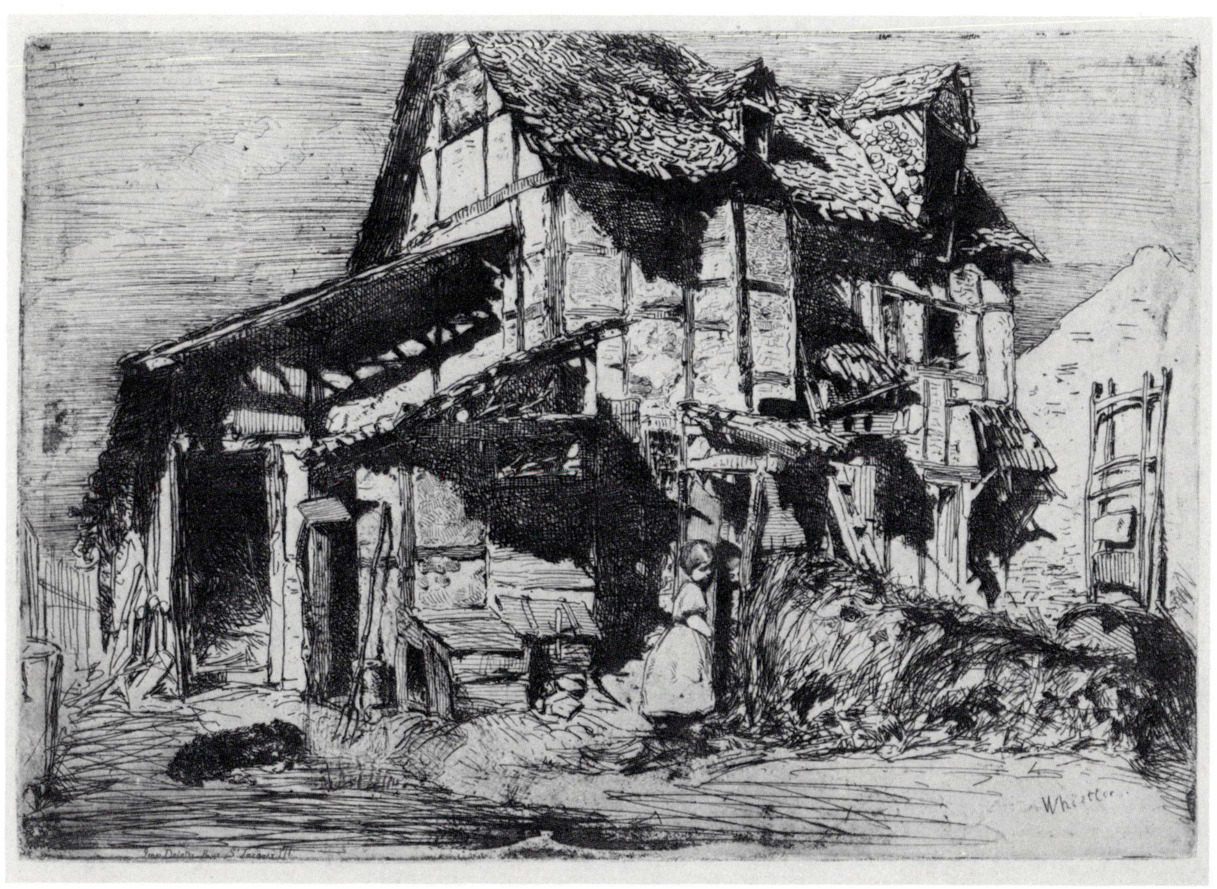

Maxime Lalanne.

37 *At Cusset, Trip to Vichy (A Cusset, Excursion de Vichy).*
Etching, undated. 4 x 5-1/2 inches (10.2 x 14 cm.).
Béraldi number 9. Collection of Dr. and Mrs. Gabriel P. Weisberg, Cleveland.

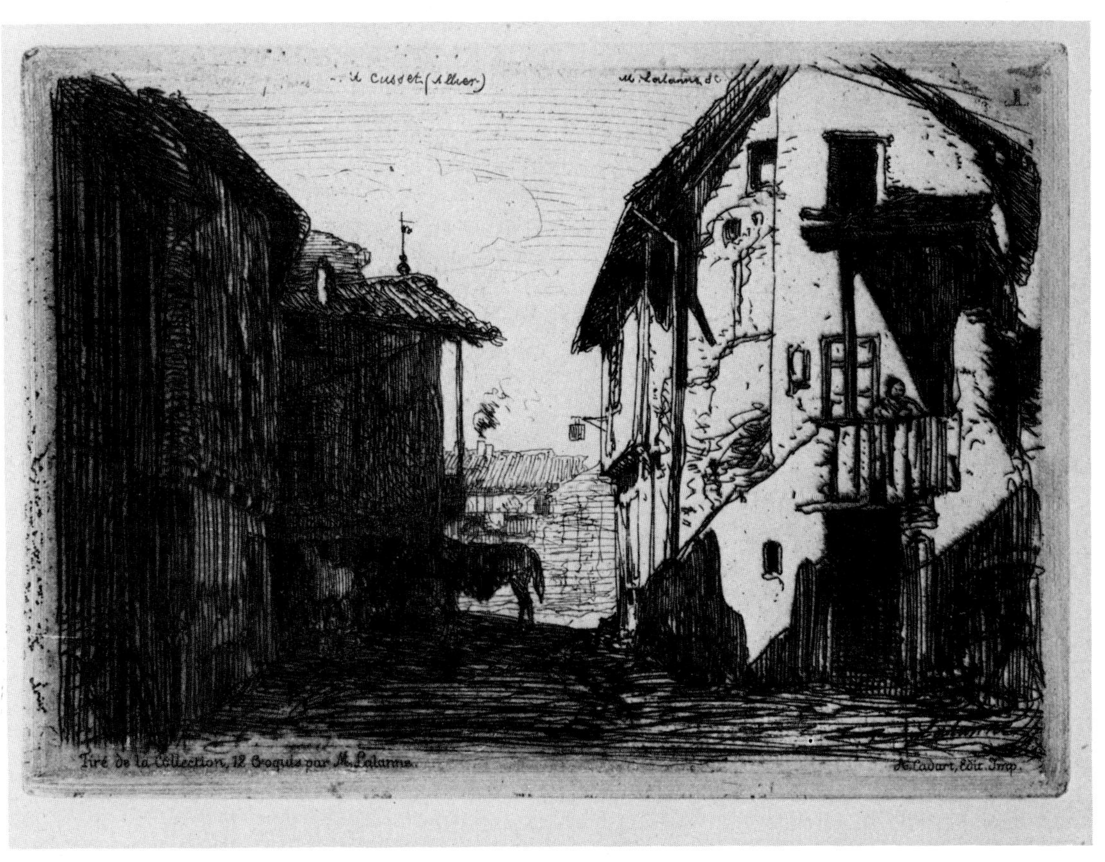

John Taylor Arms.

38 *Old Corner, Rouen.*
Etching, 1925.
6 x 4 inches
(15.2 x 10.2 cm.).
American Etchers,
Volume V, number 100.
Gift of Leona
E. Prasse.
CMA 57.375

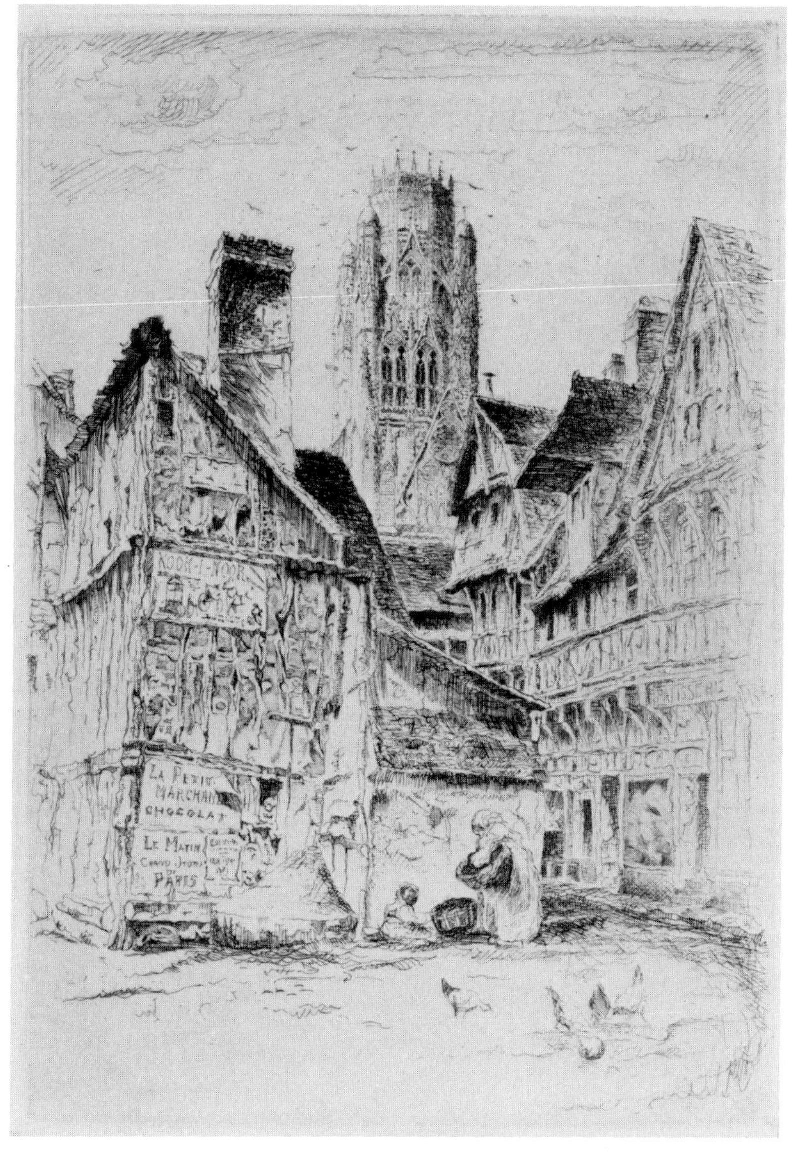

John Taylor Arms.

39 *Old Saumur, Houses
in the Rue Dacier.*
Etching, 1916.
10-1/8 x 6-1/8 inches
(25.7 x 15.5 cm.)
American Etchers,
Volume V, number 8.
Lent by Associated
American Artists,
New York.

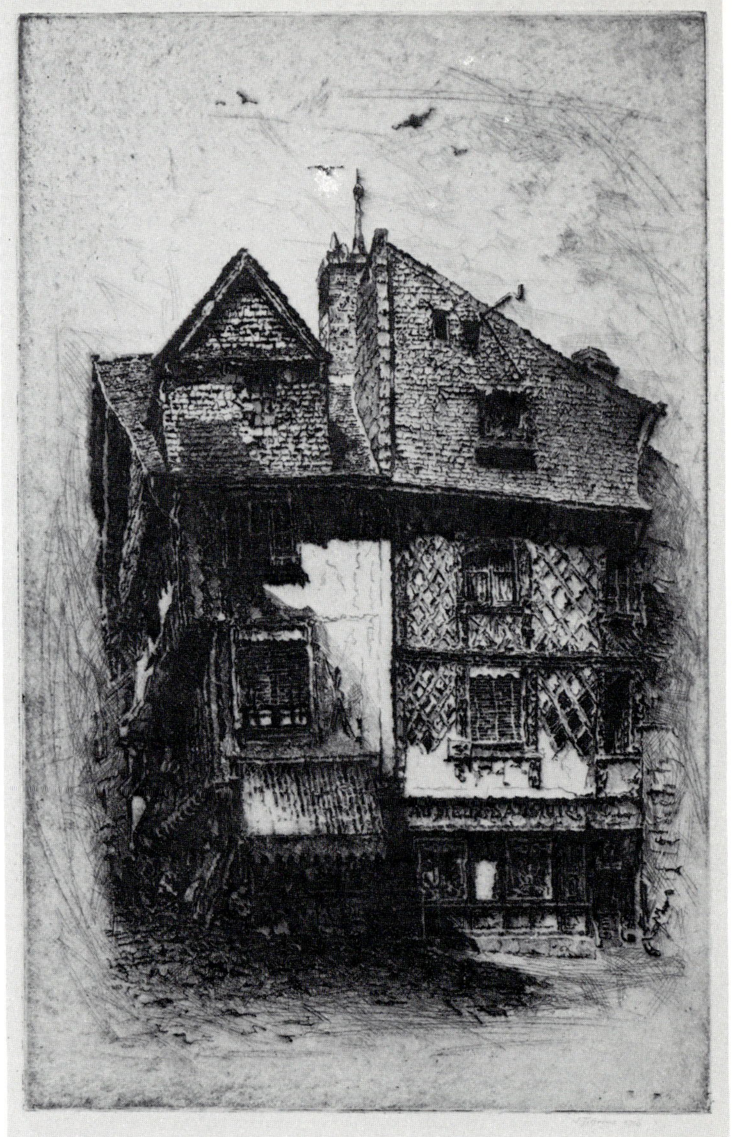

John Taylor Arms.

40 *Via Facchini, Pisa.*
Etching, 1927.
11-3/8 x 5-1/2 inches
(28.9 x 14 cm.).
American Etchers,
Volume V, number 125.
Lent by Associated
American Artists,
New York.

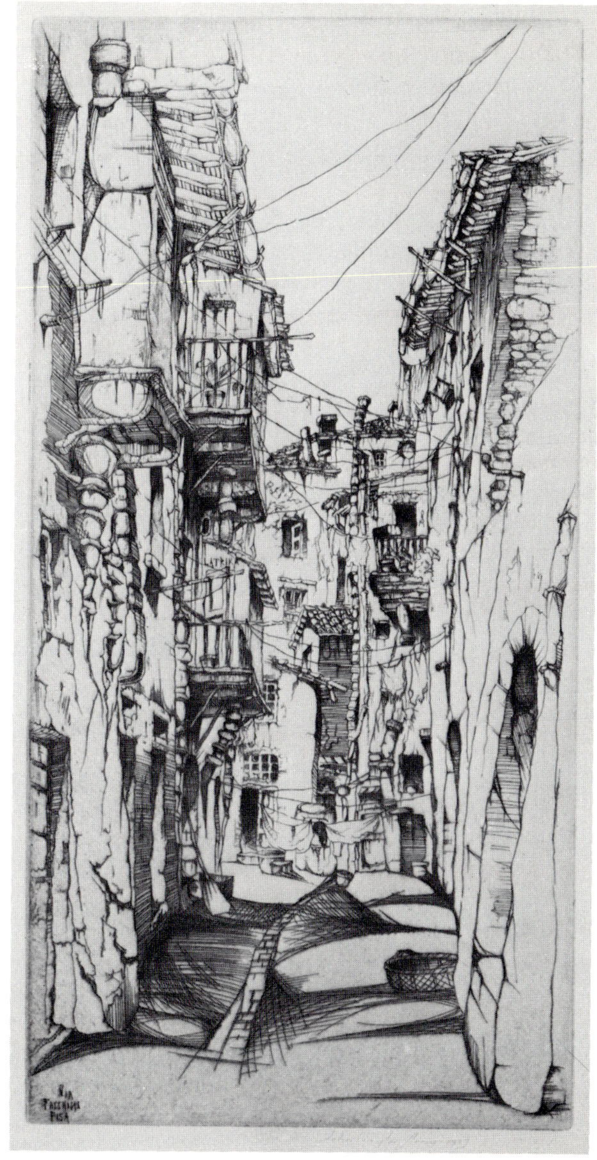

John Taylor Arms.

41 *A Tower of Saint Front,*
Perigueux.
Etching, 1928.
11-7/8 x 5-1/2 inches
(30.2 x 14 cm.).
American Etchers,
Volume V, number 138.
Lent by Associated
American Artists,
New York.

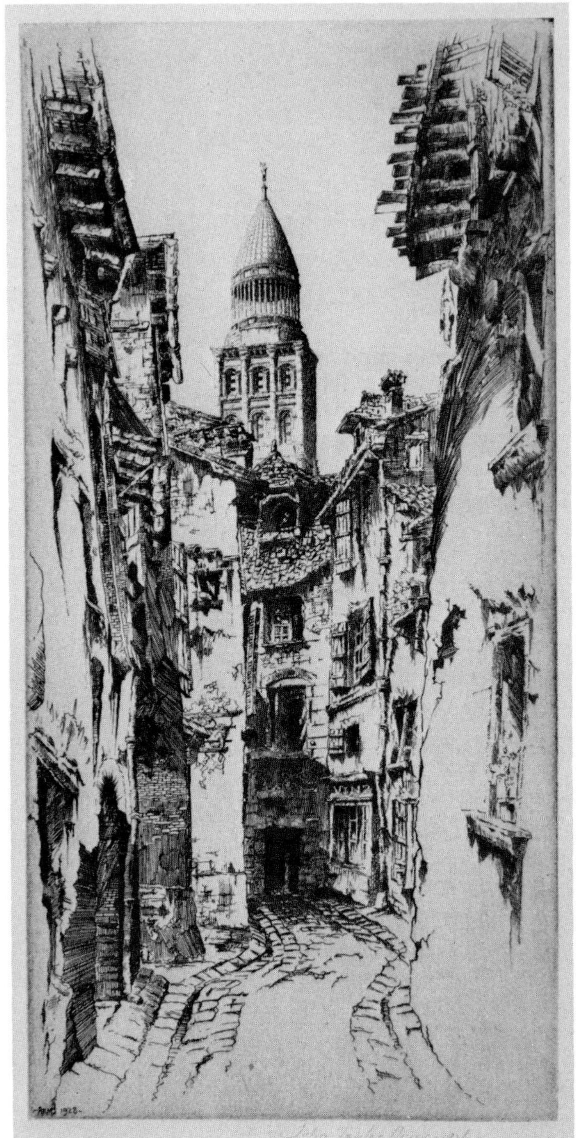

John Taylor Arms.

42 *The Cabin in the Woods.*
Etching, 1920. 5 x 7 inches (12.7 x 17.8 cm.).
American Etchers, Volume V, number 32. Lent by Associated American Artists, New York.

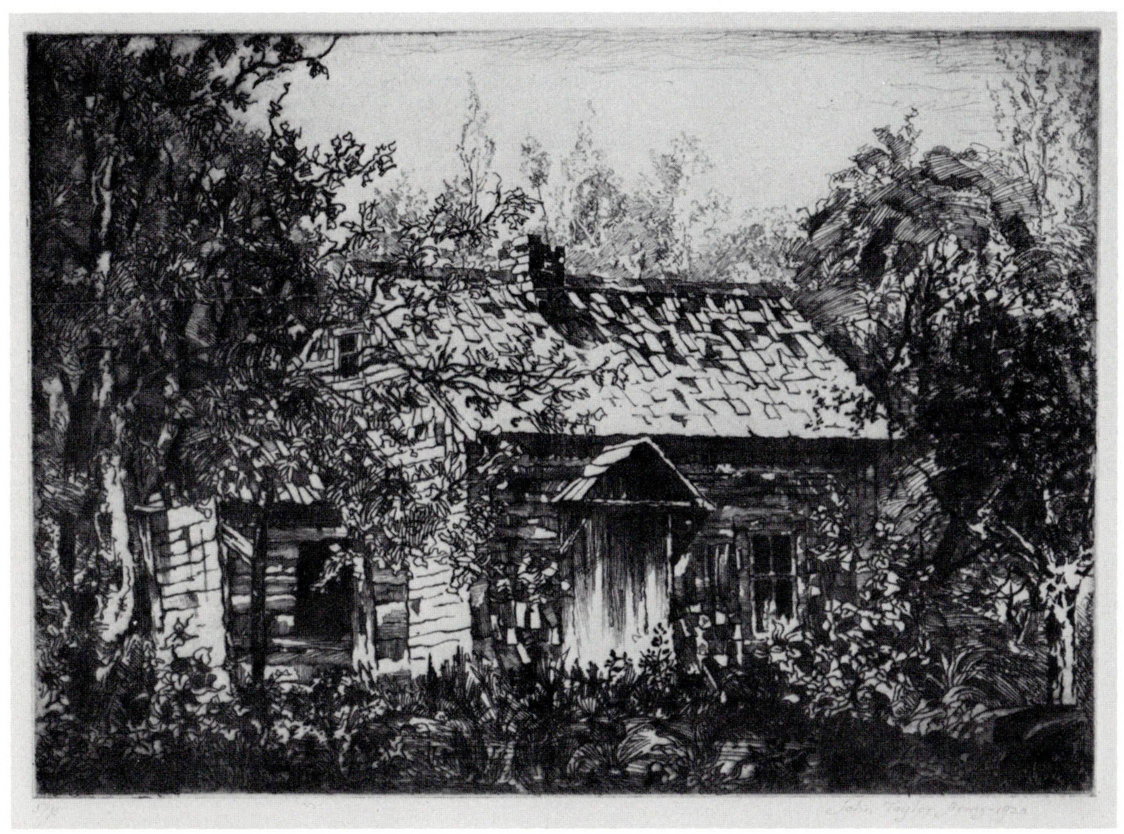

John Taylor Arms.

43 *The Red Mill.*
Etching, 1921.
11 x 7-1/8 inches
(27.9 x 18.1 cm.).
American Etchers,
Volume V, number 77.
Lent by Associated
American Artists,
New York.

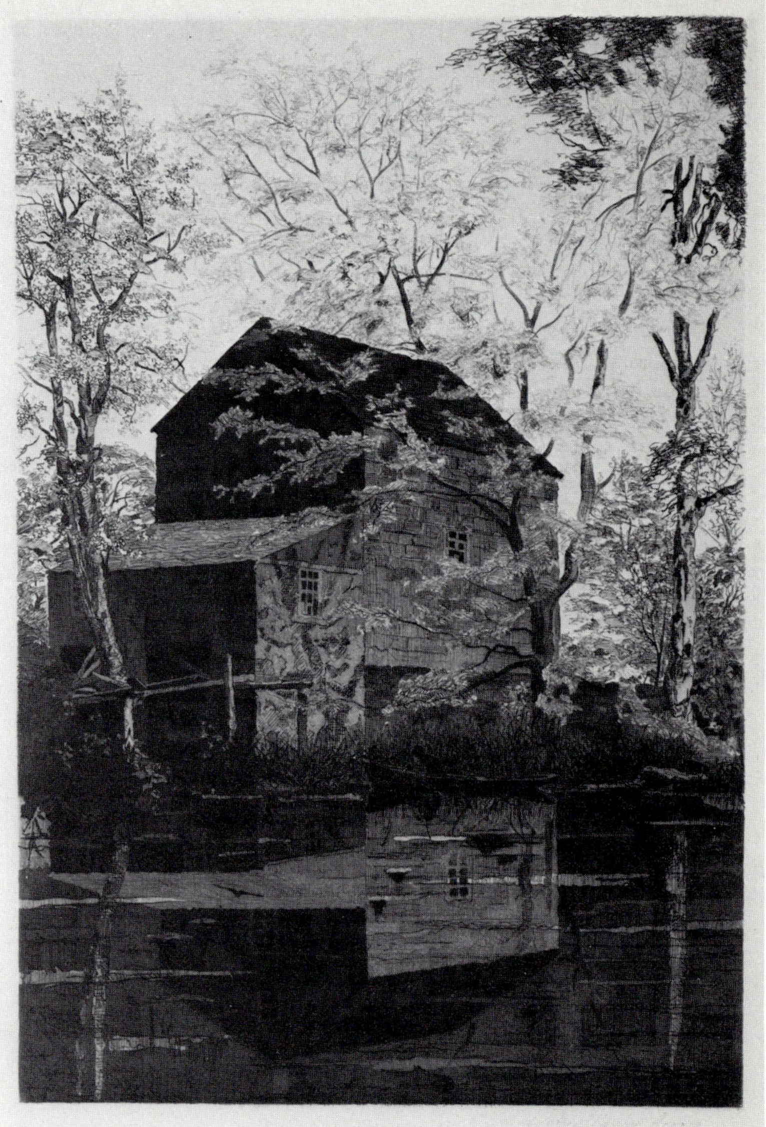

II. ENVIRONMENT: PAST AND PRESENT

C. City Streets

Aside from contemplating the monuments in a city or the picturesque locales of smaller villages, printmakers tried to change their focus to the life of a city—the activity that took place on its streets, the sense of energy that emanated from the meetings and trips that people took within their own constructed space. While few printmakers were able to record the modern tempo, some did present panoramic images which showed the life of the streets. Occasionally a printmaker would pull back from this type of examination to show solitary figures trying to find a moment of repose in the midst of an increased pace.

Maxime Lalanne in *Rue des Marmousets (Vieux Paris)* [44] was among the first to show the daily life of the city, with figures strolling along the cobblestone pavement carrying baskets or bundled in shawls as if they were tending to their activities. When James McNeill Whistler focused on the bustle of urban life in *St. James Street* [45], London, he recorded the presence of rapidly moving carriages and figures running about. The tempo is markedly increased when compared with the quieter pace that Lalanne recorded.

John Marin (1870-1953), an American artist in Paris at the turn of the century [46], found the left bank to his liking; he had the opportunity to indulge in cafe discussions among the younger artists. Here he also recorded the older buildings of the city in an attempt to find a peaceful corner where he could escape from the tensions of contemporary life.

It was not, however, until D.Y. Cameron and John Taylor Arms did their prints of *The Rialto,* 1900 [47]; *Kingsgate, Winchester,* 1902 [48]; or a *Street in Blois* [49] that one could see how important it was for artists in the twentieth century to show the contrast between the active and contemplative moods possible in an urban situation. Loneliness, alienation, and personal meditation seem to be the basic themes stressed by Arms as he related his images to past romantic traditions in an effort to underscore melancholy thoughts.

CONCLUSION

The nineteenth century was a period of rapid industrialization and urban development which brought with it problems of displacement both in the rural areas of countries and within cities. Often artists working in a very intimate medium—such as etching—reacted to the encroaching alienation of their spirits by seeking escape in nature or in meditating on monuments and villages which demonstrated a continuation of the past into the present. While the century reflected this dialogue between what could be revived and what spoke of contemporary modes, some printmakers in the twentieth century also felt isolated by the cold, mechanistic environment which left them little opportunity to commune with nature or themselves.

Seeking quiet locales, out-of-the-way corners or lonely passageways, and often meditating on Gothic monuments, printmakers revived a mode of thinking which one might have thought alien to the abstractions of the twentieth century. Some longed for an escape into previous times, and created landscapes and city views which emphasized the separation of man from his own world. It seems only a small matter to recognize how the printmakers of the nineteenth century assured the continuation of this long-standing thematic tradition for our own era.

Maxime Lalanne.

44 *Rue des Marmousets
(Vieux Paris)*.
Etching, 1863.
9-5/8 x 6-9/16 inches
(24.4 x 16.6 cm.).
Béraldi number 1.
Gift of Frederick
Keppel and Co., Inc.
CMA 18.94

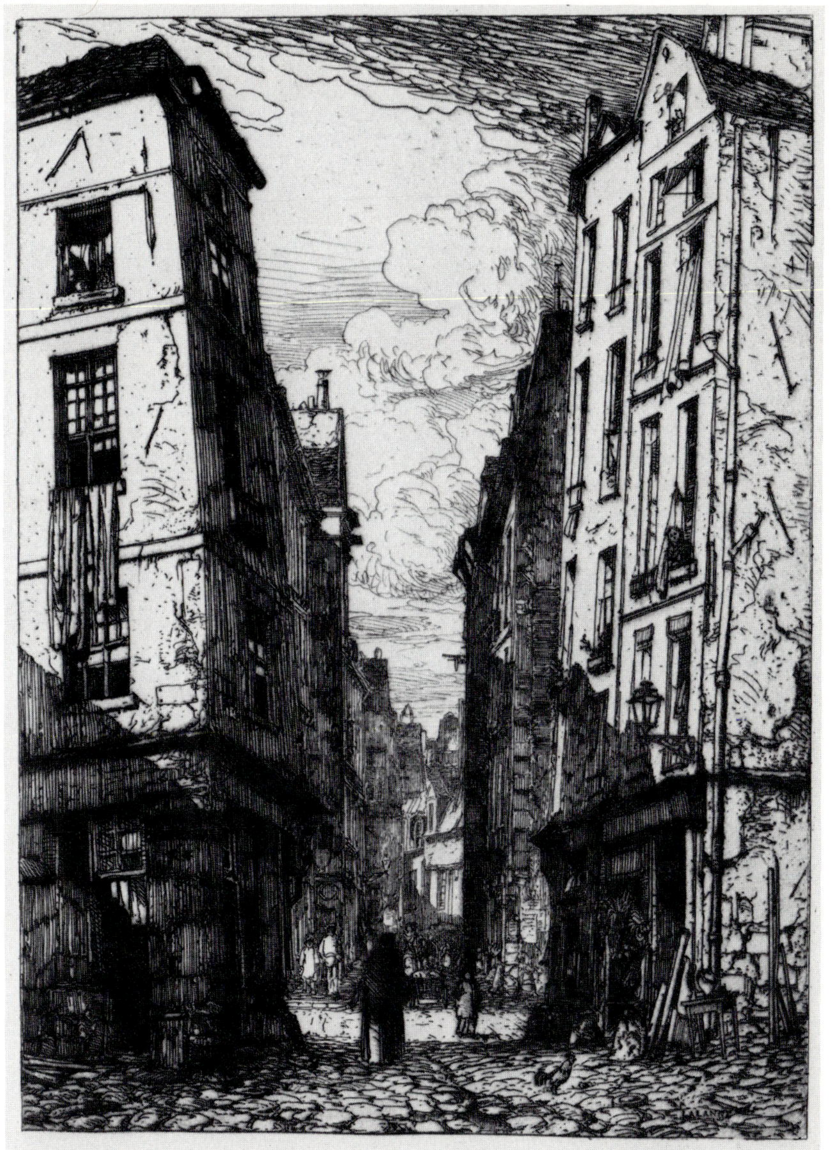

James Abbott McNeill Whistler.

45 *St. James Street.*

Etching, undated.
10-7/8 x 5-7/8 inches
(27.6 x 14.9 cm.).
Kennedy number 169, iv.
Gift of Mr. and Mrs.
Ralph King.
CMA 24.62

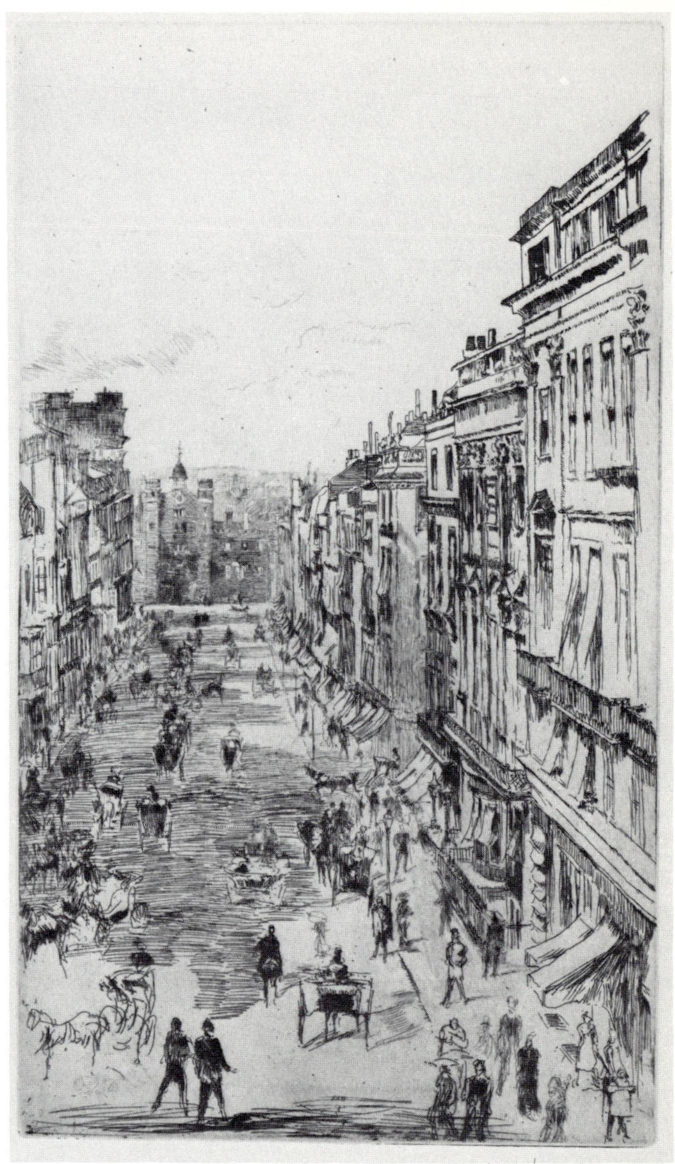

John Marin.

46 *St. Gervais, Rue Grenier
sur l'Eau, Paris.*
Etching, 1909.
9-13/16 x 7-7/8 inches
(23.3 x 20 cm.).
Zigrosser number 83.
Lent by Associated
American Artists,
New York.

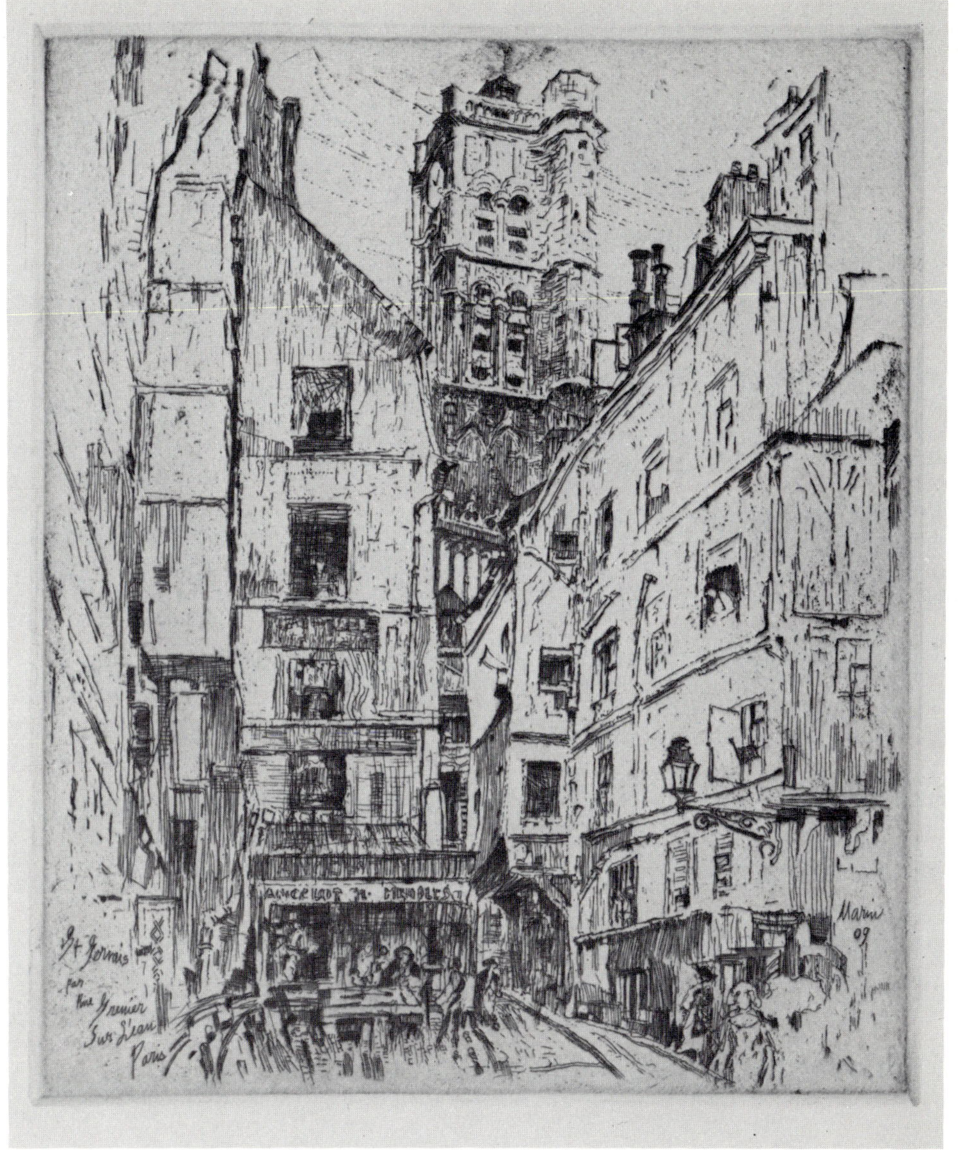

D. Y. Cameron.

47 *The Rialto*.
Etching and Drypoint, 1900.
12 x 8-3/8 inches
(30.5 x 21.2 cm.).
Rinder number 305, ii.
Lent by The College
of Wooster.

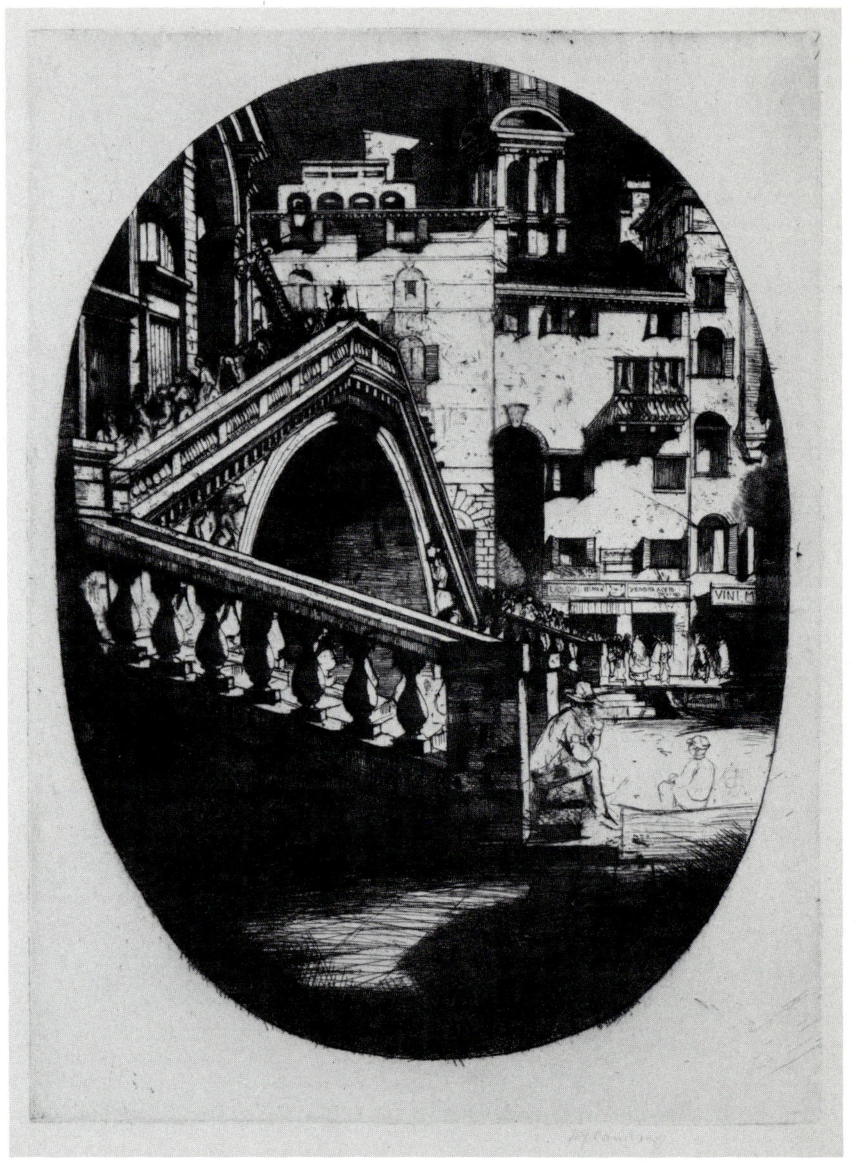

D. Y. Cameron.

48 *Kingsgate, Winchester.*
Etching, 1902.
6-7/32 x 4 inches
(15.8 x 10.2 cm.).
Rinder number 340.
Lent by The College
of Wooster.

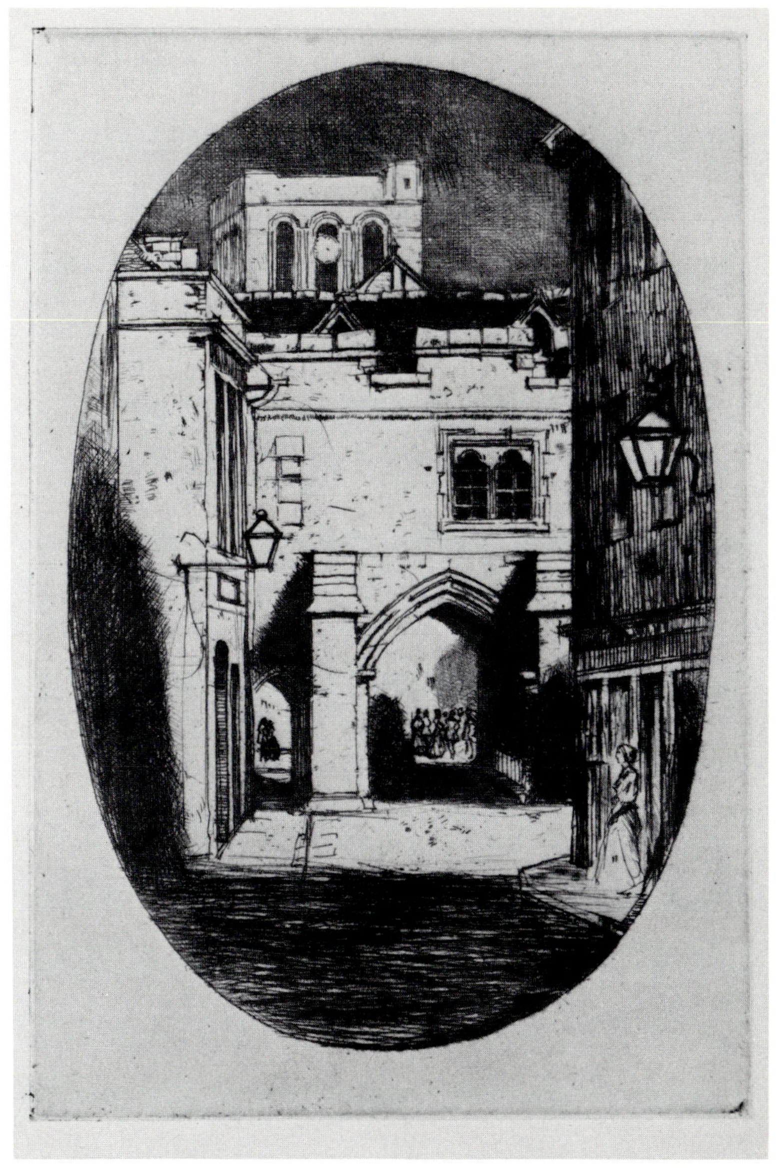

John Taylor Arms.

49 *Street in Blois*.
Etching, 1927.
7 x 5 inches
(17.8 x 12.7 cm.).
New York Public
Library number 206.
Gift of The Print Club.
CMA 33.234

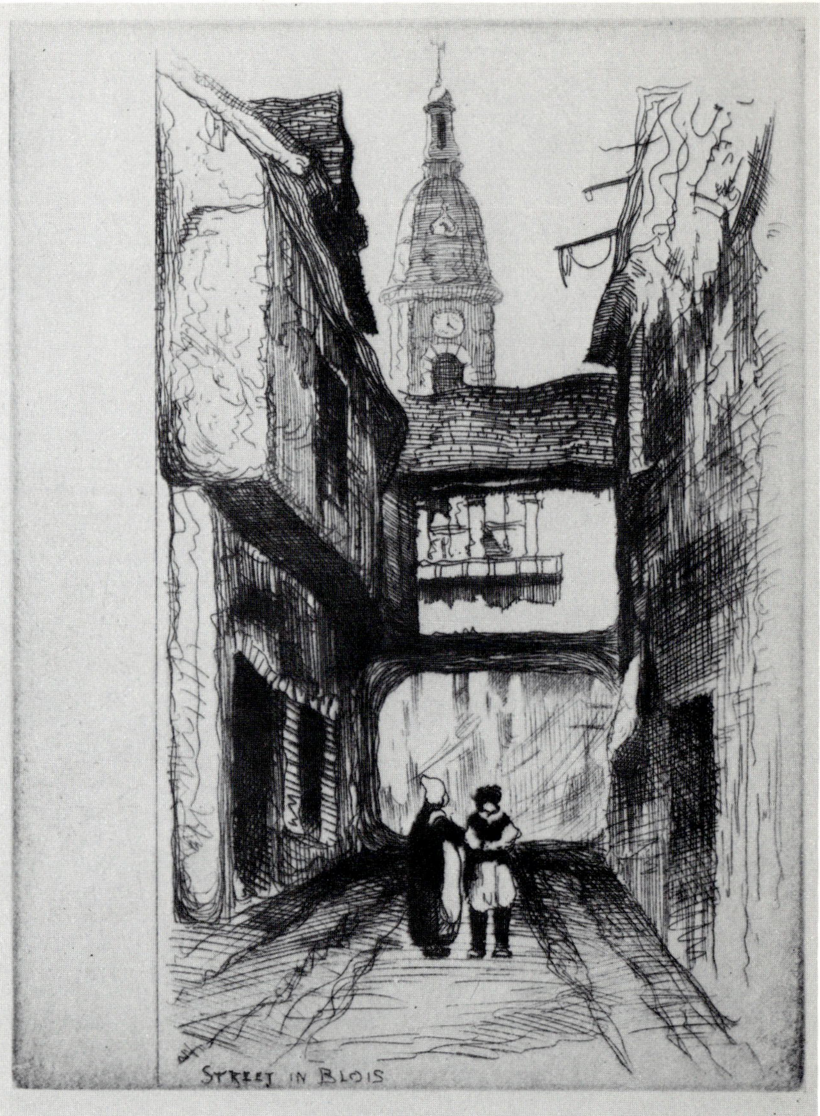

BIOGRAPHIES

Adolphe Appian (1818-1898)

Lyon, France, was an ever-present force in the life and career of painter-printmaker Adolphe Appian. He was born there in 1818 and studied painting at the Ecole des Beaux-Arts. The success and renown he established in this region, moreover, enabled him to go to Paris, where he studied the art of Corot and Daubigny and came into contact with *au-courant* artistic developments. In the early 1860's, however, when the etching revival burgeoned in the French capital with fervor and excitement, Appian was back in Lyon, experimenting on his own with the medium, at first tentatively but soon with increasing skill and assurance.

Appian's oeuvre of about 100 etchings is indeed notable—if not for its volume, certainly for its quality—and his prints were regularly published in the annual albums of the Société des Aquafortistes, established by Alfred Cadart in 1862. The artist's sense of line and draughtsmanship was perfectly attuned to the etching medium. A painterly sensibility also found expression in his prints, not only in his taste for tonal gradations of light and dark but also in his techniques: he would often rework an oil canvas in etching.

Devotion to his native town did not constrain Appian from travel. In the early 1870's he journeyed to the southwest coast of France and to Italy, returning with a wealth of visual material to Lyon, where he lived and worked until his death in 1898. In this lifelong identity with his birthplace, however, Appian was hardly a provincial. His poetic view of nature, suffused with idyllic sentiment, coincided not only with the vision of many of his artist-compatriots but also with universal impulses in printmaking in the latter half of the nineteenth century.

For specific works by Adolphe Appian, see catalogue numbers 4 and 5.

Selected Bibliography:

Curtis, Atherton and Prouté, Paul. *Adolphe Appian son oeuvre gravé et lithographié.* Paris, 1968.

Jennings, Herbert H. "Adolphe Appian" *Print-Collector's Quarterly* 12 (February 1925): 94-117.

John Taylor Arms (1887-1953)

John Taylor Arms was born in Washington, D.C. in 1887. He trained and worked as an architect, joining the firm of Carrère and Hastings in 1912. A love of draughtsmanship led him to produce his first etching in 1914, and the following year he embarked upon printmaking as a lifetime career.

Arms' earliest series of etchings—devoted primarily to picturesque, often sectional views of houses and buildings—date from 1915 to about 1920. In this period he used line freely, almost impressionistically, to capture evanescent effects of light and shadow. A more exact, meticulous technique evolved with Arms' concentration on architectural themes and motifs onward from 1920. This phase began with the "Gargoyle Series," in which Arms, in the spirit of his predecessor Charles Meryon, brought to life what he characterized as "those queer, grim grotesques, often humorous, sometimes tragic and always entirely fascinating, which constitute such telling decorative accents on all the great Gothic buildings in France."

This close study of architectural detail led Arms, inevitably it would seem, to record painstakingly the great Gothic churches of Europe, to give expression to their essential spirit. In the decade 1920-1930, Arms traveled in Spain, France, and Italy and celebrated through the faithful language of his line the Gothic style which for him represented architecture's highest achievement, combining, in his own words, "all that was most beautiful in man-made building—grandeur of scale, beauty of proportion and abundant wealth of detail." Such edifices were a continued source of inspiration to Arms until his death in 1953. During this last phase he not only re-dedicated himself to Gothic themes, but extended his imagery to interpret past and present in England, New York, and Venice.

Arms was an important and consistent spokesman for printmaking, and he strengthened considerably the continued force of this medium into the twentieth century. Beginning in 1919, he participated in public demonstrations on the etching technique. He was at one time president of the Society of American Etchers. His *Handbook on Printmaking and*

Printmakers was published in 1934, and in 1940 he became a contributing editor to the magazine *Print*. This record of public achievement viewed together with Arms' ouevre of 440 prints produced over the course of his career shows the breadth, creativity, and energy of this twentieth-century American romantic.

For specific works by John Taylor Arms, see catalogue numbers 8, 9, 10, 24, 25, 26, 27, 28, 33, 34, 35, 38, 39, 40, 41, 42, 43, and 49.

Selected Bibliography:

American Etchers. Vol. V. *John Taylor Arms.* New York, 1930.
Bassham, Ben L. *John Taylor Arms, American Etcher.* Madison: Elvehjem Art Center, 1975.
Galleries of Kennedy and Company. *John Taylor Arms, Selected Examples from Thirty Years of Etching.* New York, 1945.
Georgia Museum of Art. "John Taylor Arms, Thirty-Nine Years of Etched Memory." *Bulletin,* Winter-Spring 1975.
New York Public Library. "A Descriptive Catalogue of the Work of John Taylor Arms." 2 vols. New York, 1962. (Typewritten.)
Weisberg, Gabriel P. "Twentieth-Century Gothic: John Taylor Arms." *Art News* 75 (March 1976): 58-59.

Félix Bracquemond (1833-1914)

Félix Bracquemond was one of the central figures of the etching revival in France in the second half of the nineteenth century; his contribution was manifold. He was an important printmaker, distinguished for numerous landscape scenes and animal and portrait studies. He also championed the etching cause and the tradition of the *peintre-graveur,* and was instrumental in raising the status of the printmaker from craftsman to fine artist. As a teacher and advisor, moreover, he came into contact with artists like Manet, Degas, and Daubigny and encouraged them to venture into printmaking.

Bracquemond was born in Paris in 1833. His accomplishment in etching was rapid. At the age of fifteen he was apprenticed to a lithographer. He later studied painting and etching with Guichard (a former student of Ingres), and by the age of twenty had completely mastered the etching technique. During the course of his career he was prolific. By his death in 1914, he had produced over 900 prints and had earned many laurels—most notable among them the Medal of Honor at the Salon of 1884 and a Grand Prize at the "Exposition Universelle" in 1900.

Bracquemond's landscape etchings are among the most sensitive and refined works in his oeuvre. On his plates the image of man in nature, envisioned one generation before by the Barbizon artists, gives way to the supremacy of nature herself. This tendency more widely reflected the aims of the contemporary French Impressionists, with whom Bracquemond shared an interest in atmosphere, weather, and ephemeral qualities of light. His devotion to nature and his penchant for travel transcended national boundaries, thereby identifying his art with the broader aims of European printmakers of the time.

For specific works by Félix Bracquemond, see catalogue numbers 1, 2, and 13.

Selected Bibliography:

Weisberg, Gabriel P. "Félix Bracquemond and the Molding of French Popular Taste." *Art News* 75 (September 1976): 64-66.
Weitenkampf, Frank. "Félix Bracquemond, an Etcher of Birds." *Print-Collector's Quarterly* 2 (February-April 1912): 207-223.

D. Y. Cameron (1865-1945)

D. Y. Cameron, born in Glasgow, Scotland, in 1865, trained as an artist at the Edinburgh School of Art. Through a local collector he was introduced to the etchings of Francis Seymour Haden, who was to become an enduring influence. The works of James McNeill Whistler and Charles Meryon also sparked the imagination of the aspiring artist.

Cameron began his own career as a painter and printmaker around 1887, and from 1888 to 1902 he contributed regularly to the annual exhibitions of the Society of Painter-Etchers. His works were widely acclaimed: his appointment in 1911 as an Associate-Engraver of the Royal Academy was only one of many laurels he accrued before his death in 1945.

Cameron's etchings treat both landscape and architectural themes; it is the latter that the artist particularly relished. This taste for architecture intensified around 1900 and spurred Cameron to travel to Holland, Italy, Belgium, France, Egypt, and England in search of the picturesque.

The Rialto (cat. no. 47), a Venetian subject, shows Cameron's interest in decorative effects in its wealth of detailed line, vivid contrasts of light and dark; and its oval, almost emblematic, format. Another print, *Saint Germain l'Auxerrois,* (cat. no. 31)—published in 1904 as part of the "French Set"—is more atmospheric and suggestive in its handling of line and form. It affirms that Cameron was equally stirred by the expressiveness of architecture and sought to invoke something of its past associations—a sensibility anticipating the vision of such later, twentieth-century printmakers as John Taylor Arms.

For specific works by D.Y. Cameron, see catalogue numbers 7, 31, 32, 47, and 48.

Selected Bibliography:
Hind, Arthur M. *The Etchings of D.Y. Cameron.* London, 1924.
Rinder, Frank. *D.Y. Cameron.* Glasgow, 1912.

Frank Duveneck (1848-1933)

Duveneck is known primarily as a painter, and his reputation was largely established abroad. Born in Covington, Kentucky, in 1848, he went to Munich at the age of twenty-one to study at the Academy of Fine Arts. In 1878 he founded his own school; a year later he and his students—the so-called Duveneck Boys—moved to Italy, where they remained together as a group until 1881, spending winters in Florence and summers in Venice.

It is in Venice around 1880 that Duveneck first took up etching, under the tutelage of Otto Bacher, one of his own pupils. Around this time, too, several of Duveneck's earliest etchings were submitted to the opening exhibition of the Society of Painter-Etchers at the Hanover Gallery in London. There they attracted much praise and considerable attention, especially because they were mistaken by many for etchings by James McNeill Whistler!

Duveneck's presence in Venice did indeed coincide with Whistler's stay here, and both artists shared not only each other's acquaintance, but also a taste for similar subjects and views. This constituted, however, little basis for the above confusion which one contemporary American printmaker—Joseph Pennell—rightly found "incredible." Whistler's technique was delicate and impressionistic, his prints small and intimate. Duveneck, on the other hand, tended towards large plates and sought broad, vigorous effects of light, shadow, and line—a sensibility very much at one with the characteristic breadth and bravura of his rich and robust style of painting.

All thirty-three of Duveneck's known etchings date from 1880 to about 1885, a period during which he continued to paint. Interestingly, his canvasses from these years show a marked smoothing out of technique and lightening of palette. This change in style may reflect not only the Venetian climate and locale but also the disciplining effects of etching. After 1885 Duveneck ceased working in the latter medium and devoted the rest of his career to painting. He returned to America in 1888 and settled in Cincinnati, Ohio, where he resided until his death in 1933.

For specific works by Frank Duveneck, see catalogue numbers 15 and 16.

Selected Bibliography:
Cincinnati Art Museum. *Frank Duveneck.* Cincinnati, 1936.
Duveneck, Josephine W. *Frank Duveneck, Painter-Teacher.* San Francisco, 1970.

Francis Seymour Haden (1818-1910)

Francis Seymour Haden, born in London in 1818, was a practicing surgeon who took up etching as diversion, later to become an important printmaker well known in English and French artistic circles. His first etchings, dated 1842-43, were based on notebook sketches made on a trip to Italy. Within a few years Haden was deeply committed to the medium, encouraged, no doubt, by his brother-in-law, James McNeill Whistler. Whistler dedicated his own early plates of *Twelve Etchings after Nature* (the "French Set") to Haden and was a strong and persistent influence.

Haden, however, early developed etching in his own unique style and direction. In his prints he eschewed images of mankind, preferring instead to render intimate portraits of places—whether river scenes, countryside, or woodlands. This desire to be close to nature led him to draw directly onto the copper plate, often in drypoint, in the out-of-doors. His first etching from nature, using this manner of working, dates from 1859.

Haden's vivid use of line and the spontaneous quality of his vision attracted the attention of the English art critic and connoisseur Philip Hamerton, who found Haden's *Shere Mill Pond* (cat. no. 6) to be "with the single exception of one plate by Claude *(Le Bouvier)*, the finest etching of a landscape subject that has ever been executed in the world." Another supporter, Philippe Burty, praised Haden in 1864 in the *Gazette des Beaux-Arts* and two years later published thirty of his etchings under the title *Etudes à l'eau-forte*.

Recognition continued well into Haden's career. He was twice awarded the Grand Prix at the Paris International Exhibition—in 1889 for his etchings, and in 1900 for his mezzotints. Toward the end of his lifetime he abandoned printmaking; but he continued to be a vital force in the medium through the Society of Painter-Etchers, which he had founded in 1880 and presided over until his death in 1910.

For specific work by Francis Seymour Haden, see catalogue number 6.

Selected Bibliography:

Harrington, H.N. *The Engraved Work of Seymour-Haden.* Liverpool, 1910.
Salaman, Malcolm C. *The Etchings of Francis Seymour-Haden, P.R.E.* London, 1923.

Maxime Lalanne (1827-1886)

Maxime Lalanne was one of the rare nineteenth-century printmakers whose etchings treated both country and urban views. His special forte was the city image, as the overwhelming success and popularity of his first etching, the *Rue des Marmousets* (cat. no. 44), dated 1863 affirms. In this print, too, Lalanne's innate faculty for incisive line makes its appearance, as does his ability to capture the essence of his subject matter and its salient detail.

Lalanne's taste for the surety and clarity of line underscores his love of "pure" etching. It is this latter sensibility which no doubt gave rise to his *Treatise on Etching*, an important and far-reaching text published in 1866. Lalanne's own technical and artistic expertise earned him a medal at the Salon that same year; he had the further distinction of being the first artist ever to receive knighthood for his etching merits. This honor was conferred upon Lalanne by Ferdinand, King of Portugal, who himself indulged in the printmaking vogue, attesting once

again to the widespread force of the etching revival at this time.

Born in Bordeaux in 1827, Lalanne had first been sent to Paris to study with the historical painter Jean Gigoux. But Lalanne's artistic aspirations and endeavors were far from academic. His oeuvre of about 157 etchings, produced over a career that lasted until his death in 1886, shows that Lalanne recast the traditional aims of history painting by treating the contemporary cityscape and country scene, to document on copper plate their thriving present or crumbling past.

For specific work by Maxime Lalanne, see catalogue numbers 3, 12, 14, 20, 37, and 44.

Selected Bibliography:

Bradley, William A. "Maxime Lalanne." *Print-Collector's Quarterly* 3 (February 1913): 70-85.
Lalanne, Maxime. *A Treatise on Etching.* Boston, 1880.

John Marin (1870-1953)

John Marin, born in Rutherford, New Jersey, in 1870, was a renowned painter, printmaker, and watercolorist. As a youth, he studied both at the Pennsylvania Academy of Fine Arts and the Art Students League in New York. The turning point for his career, however, occurred with his trip to Paris in 1905. It was then and there, at the age of thirty-five, that Marin took up etching. His mastery of the medium was almost immediate, and over the next two years he produced about sixty plates, devoted primarily to picturesque sites in and around Paris.

In 1907 Marin spent six weeks in Venice, following in the wake of James McNeill Whistler, whose etching activities there anticipated his own by a little over a quarter century. Whistler inspired Marin: Marin's twenty Venetian etchings (cat. no. 17) share Whistler's taste both for the animated vignette and for impressionist intangibles of light and movement. Marin's style and sensibility, however, were totally his own. His handling was vibrant and passionate where Whistler's was delicate, decorative, and refined. An interest in structure and buildings further distinguished Marin's prints and reflected his earliest training as an architect.

Within a few years Marin's graphic style had undergone deep changes, as evidenced in his European etchings that date from 1909. *St. Gervais, Rue Grenier Sur L'Eau* (cat. no. 46) affirms the increasing force and richness of line in his work. Marin extended this new vision on his return to America in 1911, finding it an eminently suitable vehicle for recording the New York skyscrapers and bridges about him. An energetic urban imagery continued to inspire the artist, and his final New York plates date from 1930 and 1931. By that time, however, Marin's interest in printmaking had greatly waned. In the next two years he produced his last etchings, directing his attention instead to watercolor, a medium that was to occupy him, for the most part, until his death in 1953.

For specific works by John Marin, see catalogue numbers 17 and 46.

Selected Bibliography:

Zigrosser, Carl. *The Complete Etchings of John Marin.* Philadelphia, 1969.

Charles Meryon (1821-1868)

Charles Meryon was a visionary whose architectural and cityscape etchings are among the most compelling images in nineteenth-century French art. In his work, the artist gave expression to the character of his times—in particular, to France's urbanism, preoccupation with Gothic and strong romantic tendencies. At the same time, Meryon's art bodied forth his own emotional intensities. This subjective sensibility, combined with an otherwise dispassionate interest in objective nature, made his work unique, highly complex, and provocative.

Meryon was born in Paris in 1821. Between 1842 and 1846 he served in the French Navy, where his experience as midshipman and draughtsman no doubt sharpened his taste for meticulous, factual observation. It also stirred his interest in art, and on his return to Paris in 1847, Meryon prepared for a painting career. After his introduction to etching, however, printmaking totally absorbed him. This complete devotion to graphic media—to etching and drawing alone—distinguished him from both his predecessors and his *peintre-graveur* contemporaries.

Meryon's oeuvre is rich in the imagery of present and past. Both impulses found expression in his well-known *Etchings of Paris*, completed between 1850 and 1854 and published as a set. *The Vampire, An Arch of the Notre-Dame Bridge,* and *La Galerie Notre-Dame, Paris* (cat. nos. 31, 11, and 30, respectively), all dating from 1853, issued from this series. They show Meryon's predilection for sudden, unusual perspective lines and angles over the panoramic, straightforward views favored in traditional cityscapes. Such daring compositional devices reflected, in part, contemporary developments in photography. At the same time, these compressing yet thrusting lines expressed for Meryon the alienation yet magnetism of city life as well as his own persistent, disquieting inner feelings.

Among Meryon's small circle of devotees were some of the major literary figures of his day. The art critic and connoisseur Philippe Burty found Meryon's work "absolutely personal." Charles Baudelaire was moved by the "sharpness, the detail and the precision of his drawing," and Victor Hugo relished in Meryon's "fine imagination." By the 1860's the artist's work had attracted an ever-wider audience; many of his etchings were exhibited in the Salons between 1864 and 1867. But Meryon's career was already well into decline due to physical and psychological ailments. He died in an insane asylum in 1868, at the age of forty-seven.

For specific works by Charles Meryon, see catalogue numbers 11, 29, and 30.

Selected Bibliography:

Bradley, William A. "Charles Meryon – Poet." *Print-Collector's Quarterly* 3 (October 1913): 337-364.

Burke, James D. *Charles Meryon Prints and Drawings.* New Haven: Yale University Art Gallery, 1974.

Burty, Philippe. *Charles Meryon, Sailor, Engraver, and Etcher.* London, 1879.

Delteil, Loys and Wright, Harold J.L. *Catalogue Raisonné of the Etchings of Charles Meryon.* New York, 1924.

Joseph Pennell (1860-1926)

"Etchings are made because the artist must express himself by etching," Joseph Pennell once wrote. Such a straightforward, succinct statement affirms the force and centrality of this medium in the life and spirit of one of America's finest printmakers of the late nineteenth and early twentieth century.

Pennell, born in Philadelphia in 1860, took up etching in his youth and studied the prints of Francis Seymour-Haden and James McNeill Whistler in a local collection. Whistler was an ever-present source of inspiration; Pennell ranked him and Rembrandt as the two finest printmakers in history.

Pennell began his own career as a graphic artist in pen and ink, joining in the heyday of American periodical illustration. In the early 1880's *Century Magazine* of New York published an early series of his etchings—the "Philadelphia" plates—and sent him to Italy on assignment in 1883. Thence forward, Pennell's itinerary reflected the posture of the world artist-traveler. From a home base in London beginning in the early 1890's, Pennell journeyed to Spain, France, England, Belgium, Germany, America, and Greece. His subject matter— treating the industrial present and a classical, Renaissance, and Gothic past—was as wide in its range as was his mastery of techniques —among them etching, lithography, watercolor, and charcoal.

In London Pennell experimented with mezzotint, aquatint and sandpaper. His first attempt in mezzotint was *Wren's City* (cat. no. 19), and about this plate he wrote: "I am not ashamed of it—to try to render as well as I could Wren's realized dream, so I scraped and scraped and scraped my drawing from dark to light, and I have done what I could." This technique proved not a favorite with Pennell, as it did not afford the spontaneous effects sought by the artist.

The freedom of line and vivacity of feeling that characterize Pennell's finest work is evident in his last etchings that date from his move to New York in 1921 until his death there in 1926. This New York series celebrates edifices and skyscrapers that embodied for Pennell the potential of growth and renewal for a war-torn generation.

For specific works by Joseph Pennell, see catalogue numbers 18, 19, 21, 22, and 23.

Selected Bibliography:

Wuerth, Louis A. *Catalogue of the Etchings of Joseph Pennell.* Boston, 1928.

James Abbott McNeill Whistler (1834-1903)

Born in Lowell, Massachusetts in 1834, James Abbott McNeill Whistler was among several expatriate American artists working abroad in the latter half of the nineteenth century. Whistler's own career centered in London and Paris and spanned a fifty-year period. During that time he developed not only as a great painter and decorator but also as a skilled graphic artist: his etchings and drypoints form a significant part of his oeuvre.

Whistler learned to etch in his capacity as draughtsman for the United States Coastal and Geodetic Survey in late 1854 and early 1855. His association with the Survey was short-lived, and by the summer of 1855 he had settled in Paris to study art. Three years later his first set of prints—*Twelve Etchings from Nature* (the so-called "French Set")—was published. It was followed by prints of the Thames (later published in 1871 as the "Thames Set") and numerous portrait studies that earned Whistler a gold medal at an international exhibition in Amsterdam in 1863. By the late 1870's the artist was in Venice, Italy, having been commissioned by the Fine Art Society in London to make etched views of the city. This first "Venice Set," *Venice, A Series of Twelve Etchings,* was published in 1880 and was followed in 1886 by *A Set of Twenty-Six Etchings,* the second Venetian set.

After his return from Italy, Whistler continued his activities as a printmaker. His etchings dating from the latter half of his career are rich in London scenes as well as material drawn from trips to Belgium, Holland, and the French provinces. By the early 1890's the artist was back in Paris, using the medium to record its neighborhoods, boulevards, and shops. A growing interest in lithography and the condition of ill health, however, gradually claimed Whistler's etching endeavors, which by his death in 1903 had resulted in over 450 plates.

For specific works by James Abbott McNeill Whistler, see catalogue numbers 36 and 45.

Selected Bibliography:

Kennedy, Edward G. *The Etched Work of Whistler.* New York, 1910.
Naylor, Maria. *Selected Etchings of James A. McNeill Whistler.* New York, 1975.
Sutton, Denys. *James McNeill Whistler.* London, 1966.

**Publications of
the Art History and Education Department**

*American Japonism: Contacts Between America and Japan
1854-1910* by Carol Clark. 16 pp., 7 x 8 inches, 10 illus.,
1975.

Arms and Armor in The Cleveland Museum of Art
by Martin Linsey and Norma J. Roberts. 20 pp.,
7-1/2 x 9 inches, 49 illus., 1974.

Aspects of 19th-Century Sculpture by H. W. Janson with the
assistance of Christine Bishop, Holly Strawbridge,
Kenneth Pearson, Laurel Diznoff, Pamela Barboutis,
and Tom L. Johnson. 32 pp., 7-1/2 x 9 inches,
28 illus., 1975.

*An Introduction to American Art in The Cleveland Museum
of Art* by Celeste Adams, Rita Myers, and Adele Z.
Silver. 20 pp., 7-1/2 x 9 inches, 36 illus., 1972.

*An Introduction to The Art of Indian Asia in The Cleveland
Museum of Art* by Adele Z. Silver. 16 pp., 7-1/2 x 9
inches, 19 illus., undated.

An Introduction to The Arts of Africa and Oceania
by Emelia Sica and Evelyn Mitchell. 16 pp., 7-1/2 x 9
inches, 23 illus., 1973.

In the Nature of Materials: Japanese Decorative Arts
by Marjorie Williams. 41 pp., 8-3/4 x 11 inches, 32 illus.,
1977.

Materials and Techniques of 20th-Century Artists by Dee
Driscole, Dorothy Ross, under the guidance of Gabriel
P. Weisberg, Andrew T. Chakalis, Karen Smith, and
Jung Hargrove. 48 pp., 7-1/2 x 9 inches, 31 illus., 1976.

*Traditions and Revisions: Themes from the History of
Sculpture* by Gabriel P. Weisberg, with an Introduction
by H. W. Janson. 144 pp., 8-1/4 x 10-1/2 inches, 119
illus. (2 color), 1975. LC 75-26708, ISBN 0-910386-23-4.

*For information on ordering any of these titles or other books
about the Museum, please contact the Museum Sales Desk,
The Cleveland Museum of Art, 11150 East Boulevard,
Cleveland, Ohio 44106.*